Best Easy Day Hikes
Pinnacles National Park

D0707303

Help Us Keep This Guide Up to Date

Every effort has been made by the authors and editors to make this guide as accurate and useful as possible. However, many things can change after a guide is published—trails are rerouted, regulations change, facilities come under new management, and so forth.

We welcome your comments concerning your experiences with this guide and how you feel it could be improved and kept up to date. While we may not be able to respond to all comments and suggestions, we'll take them to heart, and we'll also make certain to share them with the authors. Please send your comments and suggestions to the following address:

Globe Pequot
Reader Response/Editorial Department
246 Goose Lane
Guilford, CT 06437

Or you may e-mail us at:
editorial@falcon.com

Thanks for your input, and happy trails!

Best Easy Day Hikes Series

Best Easy Day Hikes
Pinnacles National
Park

Linda B. Mullally and David S. Mullally

GUILFORD, CONNECTICUT
HELENA, MONTANA

FALCONGUIDES ®

An imprint of Rowman & Littlefield
Falcon and FalconGuides are registered trademarks and Make
Adventure Your Story is a trademark of Rowman & Littlefield.

Distributed by National Book Network

Copyright © 2016 by Rowman & Littlefield

Maps: Alena Joy Pearce © Rowman & Littlefield

British Library Cataloguing in Publication Information Available

Library of Congress Cataloging-in-Publication Data Available

ISBN 978-1-4930-2251-9 (paperback)
ISBN 978-1-4930-2252-6 (electronic)

Contents

Acknowledgments.. viii
Introduction... 1
How to Use This Guide 14
Trail Finder 16
Map Legend... 18

The Hikes

East Pinnacles–Hollister Gateway

1. Visitor Center to Bacon Ranch.................................... 21
2. Visitor Center to Butterfield Homestead...................... 24
3. Visitor Center to Peaks View Day Use Area 29
4. Peaks View Day Use Area to
   Bear Gulch Day Use Area....................................... 34
5. Peaks View Day Use Area to Old Pinnacles Trailhead... 39
6. Old Pinnacles Trail to Balconies Cave.......................... 44
7. Condor Gulch Trail to Overlook.................................. 49
8. Bear Gulch Trail.. 52
9. Bear Gulch Day Use Area to Lower Cave 56
10. Bear Gulch Day Use Area to Lower and Upper Caves... 60
11. Bear Gulch Day Use Area to Reservoir via Rim Trail.... 65
12. Bear Gulch Day Use Area to High Peaks 70

West Pinnacles–Soledad Gateway

13. Visitor Contact Station to Vista Point 77
14. Juniper Canyon Trail to High Peaks.............................. 80
15. Balconies Trail to Machete Ridge.................................. 85
16. Balconies Trail to Balconies Cliffs via Balconies Cave... 89
17. North Wilderness Trail to Twin Knolls.......................... 95

Hike Index.. 99
About the Authors 101

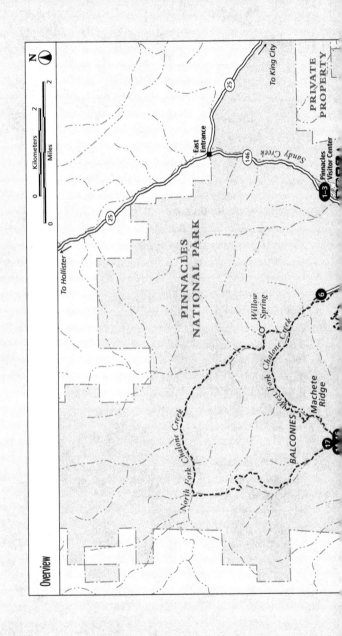

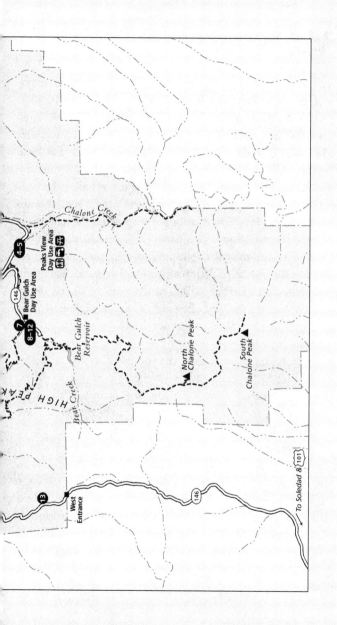

Chalone Creek

Peaks View
Day Use Area

146

Bear Gulch
Day Use Area

Bear Gulch
Reservoir

Bear Creek

HIGH PEAK

North
Chalone Peak

South
Chalone Peak

West
Entrance

146

To Soledad & 101

Acknowledgments

It was a privilege to be asked to write the first comprehensive guide to Pinnacles National Park with *Hiking Pinnacles National Park* and be trusted to do justice to Pinnacles in its debut as a national park. Most recently, putting together the "best easy day hikes" in a companion guide has been a cherished opportunity to reconnect with this amazing landscape. This companion guide would not have been possible without the resources garnered over the several months spent hiking Pinnacles National Park for the original more comprehensive guide. The park's staff, interns, and volunteers were enthusiastic about their role in polishing this new gem in the crown of national parks and eager to share their expertise and knowledge. We are grateful for their support on our mission to frame the park's beautiful ecological story and fascinating geological journey while doing justice to the cultural history.

The hiking was the easy part compared to the challenges of getting to the finish line with the first edition of *Hiking Pinnacles National Park*. We thank the team at Falcon for shepherding the editing process that has helped create two products designed to enhance visitors' experiences, whether they have an hour or a week to savor Pinnacles National Park. *Best Easy Day Hikes Pinnacles National Park*, a companion guide to *Hiking Pinnacles National Park*, arrives just in time to celebrate the one hundredth anniversary of the National Park System. To echo the sentiment expressed in Ken Burns's 2009 PBS series, Pinnacles is one more affirmation that national parks are still "America's Best Idea."

Introduction

This guide is for those with limited time to hike Pinnacles National Park, or for those who want to sample only the easiest or most popular trails. This first edition of *Best Easy Day Hikes Pinnacles National Park* was extracted from our more comprehensive guide about our newest national park (January 10, 2013), *Hiking Pinnacles National Park*, published in March 2015.

The park straddles two counties, San Benito and Monterey, in the southern portion of the Gabilan Range ecoregion, which is part of California's Central Coast Range. The park sits 80 miles south of San Francisco Bay and 40 miles inland from the Pacific Ocean and the Monterey Peninsula, a world-renown tourist destination.

The Pinnacles is a rare ecologically pristine swath of California landscape partly because of its long-standing protected status (1908), geological origins, and off-the-beaten-track access. The 30 miles of developed trails does not make Pinnacles the biggest or flashiest park, but there's a reason the crusade to protect it began so long ago.

The time line to present-day Pinnacles National Park spans millions of years of dynamic geology before humans made their imprint on the landscape. The unique "pinnacles" for which the park is named are a tale of subducting and grinding tectonic plates, volcanic fields, earthquakes, and erosion.

Simply put, the grinding and shifting of the Pacific and North American plates eventually formed California's famous San Andreas Fault, which splits the Pinnacles/Neenach volcanics. Over a period of several million years, the strike-slip motion on the San Andreas Fault has moved the two halves of the volcanic stack apart, with the prominent pinnacles moving north and leaving the rubble remnant Neenach about 200 miles south.

Other less known faults had a hand in the sculpting process as cracks created a pathway for erosion of the fissured and tilted rocks. Wind, water, heat, cold, ice, and tectonic shakes helped sculpt the landscape of towers, crags, monoliths, palisades, and canyons that continue to fascinate visitors to Pinnacles National Park. Heaps of ginormous boulders jammed in crevices and steep gorges became the ceilings to the awesome talus caves. Pinnacles has some of the most accessible talus caves in the National Park System.

Uplifts and faults continue today. Pinnacles moves northward about 1 inch per year relative to the land on the other side of the San Andreas Fault. The uplift is much slower, but marked by how the streams are cutting narrow canyons through the uplifting rocks. Fault lines and rock fractures also allow for water to percolate to the surface and create trickles called "springs" that nourish riparian pockets. Subtle but tangible evidence of dynamic geology along the San Andreas Fault can be seen when you travel to the East Entrance of Pinnacles National Park from Hollister on CA 25, where small sections of the road's painted white line are offset where the fissure traverses the pavement.

As an added bonus, the Pinnacles region's minimally acidic volcanic soil has attracted a growing number of vintners and fans of good wine.

But Pinnacles National Park is not just rock spires, boulder-stacked tunnels, and talus caves. Elevations range from 790 feet along seasonal Chalone Creek to 3,304 feet atop panoramic North Chalone Peak. The primarily dual-season Mediterranean climate, characterized by relatively cool, wet winters and hot, dry summers, nurtures the more drought-resistant vegetation mix of California chaparral. Small spiny-needle chamise dominates the chaparral shrub and brush lands mixed with manzanita and buck brush.

From March to May the rolling green grassy hills of late winter and spring become incubators for splashes of orange poppies, purple bush lupines, pink shooting stars, yellow monkey flowers, crimson Indian warriors, and a myriad of delicate wildflowers before green turns to summer gold and autumn brown.

Gray pines and blue oaks (deciduous) dot the arid summer slopes. But coast live oaks (evergreen), cottonwoods, and sycamores burgeon and huddle in the park's riparian hideaways. The buckeye's growth cycle has adapted well by flourishing in the late winter to early spring months and shedding its leaves to go dormant in the dry summer months. The deciduous valley oak, the largest oak in America, graces the banks along stretches of the Chalone Creek watershed. In sharp contrast, Pinnacles' precious few lush leafy canyons, moist mossy gorges, and spring-fed riparian islands in gravel creek beds form a necklace of natural habitats that sets off the majestic volcanic centerpiece. Almost 300 types of lichen, natural indicators of air quality, have been identified within Pinnacles National Park.

Extremes of hot summers (with highs over 100 degrees Fahrenheit daytime temperatures) and cold winters (as low as teens and 20s nighttime temperatures), along with its longtime protection as a federal public land, have acted as natural buffers preserving Pinnacles' high ratio of native plants and animals. The yellow star thistle wreaked havoc on the park's native grasslands, but the area is recovering thanks to consistent effort over the past several years using various techniques from hand pulling, hoeing, mowing, and grazing to prescribed burning and limited herbicide use.

From stealth mammalian predators (mountain lions, bobcats, and coyotes) and majestic raptors to rare amphibians and tiny insects, Pinnacles National Park provides a wide range of habitat and a model for a healthy ecosystem that helps nurture endangered species.

Imagine 70 species of butterflies, 500 species of moths, 40 species of dragonflies, and 400 types of bees taking their place in the park's ecosystem. In the air, over 170 species of birds have been documented.

In the spring and summer, birds flock to the riparian oases, while woodpeckers can be heard tapping the pines and oaks. Falcons, hawks, eagles, and owls nest and roost in the crags of cliffs. Prairie falcons breed in higher concentrations at Pinnacles than in any other National Park Service unit. Turkey vultures, carrion eaters and cousin to the larger and more rare California condor, circle the heights. Listen for the barn owl calls piercing the night air.

Fourteen of twenty-four species of California bats are found in Pinnacles. Bear Gulch Cave's lower and upper configuration and temperature range provide the Townsend's big-eared bat, listed as a "sensitive species" in California, an ideal wintering ground and a safe maternity ward to pup and raise youngsters in the warmer months. The Bear Gulch colony is known as "the largest maternity colony between San Francisco and Mexico." In order to protect the bats from being disturbed during these two critical cyclical periods of life, the talus caves are monitored for periodic seasonal closures. The schedule is updated and posted on the park's website: www.nps.gov/pinn.

After an absence of eighty years, the California condor, largest flying bird in North America, has returned to Pinnacles National Park, which is one of three condor release sites in California (two in central California and one in southern California). Breeding condors in captivity as part of an experimental program gave hope to reintroducing condors in the wild. Pinnacles National Park has been part of the condor recovery program since 2003. The park currently monitors over twenty condors, which are tagged and tracked by radio transmitters. The park partners with the Ventana Wildlife Society to ensure the survival of the endangered condors in central California. You can celebrate their return, watching them glide silently on the High Peaks' warm updrafts and sometimes perched on a rocky spire warming their outstretched wings.

The park attracts hikers, rock climbers, and bird-watchers. Campers enjoy the developed campground at the East Entrance. There is no camping at the West Entrance. The more time you spend in Pinnacles, the more you realize that the seduction goes beyond its more obvious geologic wow factor. From vertiginous to bucolic, Pinnacles displays a range of unique faces and expresses changing moods with every season. Winter rains shine the cliffs and fill the reservoir as still pools of water in the gulches turn to cascades and waterfalls. Spring sprouts shady canopies above and carpets of green with a brilliant patchwork of wildflowers under your feet. The cycle of desert to garden and brown to green that sustains the park's biodiversity never ceases to inspire and captivate the observer.

Any of the seventeen hikes described in this book will introduce you to a unique aspect of the Pinnacles realm.

The Journey to Parkhood

Native Americans thrived in California for thousands of years prior to the arrival of Europeans. Back when California was an extension of Spain's empire, twenty-one religious missions were established between 1769 and 1823, connecting San Diego north to Sonoma within one day's walk or horseback ride apart. Many of California's native peoples, including the Chalone and Mutsun of the Pinnacles region, were forced into abandoning their way of life. By the mid-1800s European disease and brutal treatment by their conquerors had decimated California's indigenous population.

Removal and death of most of the native people in the region by 1810 left the Pinnacles void of permanent human settlements until the arrival of Euro-American pioneers in 1865. By the 1880s the unusual rock outcrop (Pinnacles), then called the "Palisades," reappeared on the radar as a local destination for picnicking, camping, and exploring the caves.

In the early 1890s accounts of this enigmatic region in newspaper articles attracted the curiosity of adventuresome spirits. Schuyler Hain, a homesteader to Bear Valley (CA 25) from Michigan, began actively promoting the Pinnacles with tours to the area and through the caves. In 1906 Hain's early activism resulted in the protection of parts of Pinnacles as a forest reserve, followed by the 1908 Antiquities Act, which gave President Theodore Roosevelt the power to designate just over 2,000 acres of the scenic centerpiece as Pinnacles National Monument.

More land was consolidated into the Pinnacles National Monument during subsequent presidencies. In the 1930s the tunnel to the High Peaks was constructed and the park's infrastructure and network of trails got a real boost with a Civilian Conservation Corps (CCC) of 200 volunteers. Among the improvements were a better road up Bear Gulch, tourist cabins, a visitor center (now the seasonally open nature center in Bear Gulch), and the dam at the Bear Gulch Reservoir. The original Chalone Peak fire lookout was built in 1935, then rebuilt in 1952 following a blaze the previous year. With the exception of the nature center, most of the small original wood cabins with local stone foundations in Bear Gulch now serve as administrative offices for the national park headquarters.

In 2000, under President Bill Clinton, the 17,000-acre monument was expanded to nearly 27,000 acres. Nearly 8,000 acres of adjacent Bureau of Land Management lands were added to the monument that year. In 2006, 2,000 acres of private ranch land at the East Entrance, including historic homesteads, were acquired and consolidated into the monument. In addition to broadening the monument's ecosystem and adding another cultural dimension, the once privately owned campground became part of the monument.

Although a bill to make Pinnacles National Monument a national park was drafted around 2000, it took another tenacious ten years for it to get legislative traction. By late 2012 a park was born out of political partnerships fueled by dogged determination, and Congress approved the park bill.

On January 10, 2013, President Barack Obama signed the park bill into law, redesignating Pinnacles from national monument to national park. By the time the monument was redesignated as the country's fifty-ninth national park, Pinnacles' boundaries embraced almost 27,000 acres, 16,000 of which are designated wilderness. The Pinnacles Wilderness was renamed the Hain Wilderness in honor of Schuyler Hain. Wilderness designation assures more solitude and the privilege of time-traveling into our natural past and experiencing the land as it was and can be when you remove or minimize the presence of mankind.

By 2014 Pinnacles' new status put it in the local, national, and international spotlight, attracting 30 percent more visitors. As a result of the pressures from regional growth in recent years, increased popularity with publicized national park status, expansion of the park's territory, and other evolving ecological and logistic factors, a new General Management Plan was undertaken to consider options for balancing recreation, interpretation, and education with resource protection. The alternative adopted by the plan focuses on bringing people and nature closer together. The park welcomes over 200,000 visitors annually, with the peak traffic during March, April, and May. Parking, day-use areas, a campground, visitor centers, intrapark shuttle service, expansion of the 30-mile hiking trail network, more access to the wilderness experience, and interpretive programs are among the long list of visitor-centered topics addressed in the new General Management Plan.

In the shorter term, visitors can expect the construction of two new trails to begin in 2016. A 2.25-mile trail will connect the west-side Visitor Contact Station with the Chaparral Picnic Area parking and associated trailheads. Currently, there is only a paved road and no exclusively pedestrian access linking the station with the trailheads. The other trail is a 0.5-mile, ADA-compliant loop that will start and end at the Visitor Contact Station.

Longer-term projects being explored involve new educational and park orientation amenities centered around the historic homestead land at the east-side entrance as well as campground improvements and possible limited wilderness camping opportunities.

For park information, contact Pinnacles National Park, 5000 CA 146, Paicines, CA 95043-9770; (831) 389-4485 or (831) 389-4427; www.nps.gov/pinn.

Transportation

Pinnacles National Park is divided into the west side and the east side by its most prominent geological feature: the volcanic rampart running north and south that is known as the Pinnacles. There is no road through the park connecting the West and East Entrances. Although the map shows a section of CA 146 on each side of the park, it is *not* a through-road. The only way to access the park from west to east or east to west by road and the shortest route around is to drive south from either entrance via King City on surface roads between US 101 and CA 25.

The only transportation within the park on the west side is your vehicle.

On the east side there is a seasonal free shuttle that ferries visitors from the visitor center at the East Entrance to Bear Gulch Day Use Area. The shuttle typically runs at 30-minute intervals during peak visitor season on weekends from Presidents' Day weekend in February to Memorial Day weekend at the end of May. The shuttle may run on other holiday weekends or special events during the year. For up-to-date shuttle information, check the Twitter feed @PinnaclesNPS or the Pinnacles National Park Facebook page. Visit the park website, www.nps.gov/pinn, for updates and alerts or call (831) 389-4485.

Communication

Except for an unreliable and sporadic signal with AT&T service in the High Peaks, there is no cell service in the park. A pay phone that operates with a calling card or credit card is located outside the visitor center and campground store at the East Entrance. Your best bet in the event of an emergency is the park headquarters in Bear Gulch.

Weather

The climate is generally described as "Mediterranean," bouncing between the hot dry summers and cold moist winters. Pinnacles benefits from the tempering influence of the Pacific Ocean, but the Santa Lucia Mountains create a meteorological barrier between the park and the coast.

The Fahrenheit temperature variation between the coast (40 miles as the condor flies) can be as much as 50 degrees, especially in the summer when days can rise to 100 degrees in the park and remain in the 50s under a cloak of fog on the coast. Nighttime temperatures in the winter easily drop into the low 30s and on occasion into the 20s in the park, while the coast remains more temperate, rarely dipping to freezing.

The Santa Lucia Mountains capture most of the winter rainfall from Pacific storms, leaving the park with an annual average of about 16 inches. It is not uncommon for the higher elevations to get a dusting of white powder between December and March, when an "Arctic Express" chills the state.

Close up, there are microclimates within the park. Exposed slopes can be unbearably hot for summer hiking, but pleasant in the leafy canyons and in the moist cool of the caves. Spring northwest winds on the ridges and peaks can make you wish you had an extra layer, whereas hikers in the creek-bed canyons are stripping down to T-shirts. Although mornings can start out cold, once the sun hits the park, a warm day forecast for Hollister or Soledad can quickly turn to "hot" by a 10-degree differential in Pinnacles National Park. Check the forecast for Hollister on the east side and Soledad for the west side. Visit www.nps.gov/pinn and click on Plan Your Visit for current park alerts on weather and other crucial seasonal information.

California climate cycles between wet and dry, with flood and drought years. Pinnacles National Park suffers the brunt of these historic extremes. At the time this book was researched in 2015, California was in its fourth year of severe drought. But even with less-than-normal rainfall, the parched dusty landscape has its moment of green life with a splash of wildflower color in the spring months. Even if only momentarily, after a rainfall, water will drape sheer rock walls and creeks will surprise you with a trickle that can grow into a cascade in some gulches. All of it is a testament to the resilience of the land.

Safety and Comfort

- Wear layers to transition from cold to hot or from breezy to windy on the ridges.
- Choose footwear with ankle support and traction.
- Carry a hat with a brim, and lather up with sunscreen for sun protection.
- Always carry water to stay hydrated and snacks for energy.

- Caves require a good flashlight or headlight (cell phones and penlights won't cut it through the dark craggy caves) and steady footing.
- Take binoculars to spot condors.

Pets

Pets are not allowed on the trails. Dogs on leash are only allowed in the campground, picnic areas, and parking lots and on the paved roads. The park discourages visitors from leaving pets in a car since outdoor temperatures of 75 degrees or more can be deadly to an animal in a vehicle in a place where the temperature can rise above 100 degrees.

Camping

Camping is available at the Pinnacles Campground at the East Entrance. The campground has 99 tent sites, 39 RV sites with 30-amp electricity (water and dump station nearby), and 14 group sites. There are showers near the visitor center and several garbage and recycling containers. The campground also features an outdoor amphitheater for ranger-led campfire programs and an outdoor swimming pool, which is not heated and open seasonally from 10 a.m. to 6 p.m.

Be sure to plan ahead if you intend to camp on weekends in the spring during the wildflower spectacle. For reservations, call (877) 444-6777 or go to www.recreation.gov. The campground store telephone number is (831) 389-4538.

At this time there is no wilderness camping permitted in the park.

Park Fees

Single Visit

Vehicle or Motorcycle (valid for 5 days)	$10
Walk-In or Bicycle (valid for 7 days)	$5

Annual Pass

Pinnacles Annual Pass	$20
Interagency Annual Pass	$80

Lifetime Passes

Interagency Senior Pass (62 and over)	$10
Interagency Access Pass (disabled)	free

Leave No Trace

- Respect posted rules.
- Close gates where indicated.
- Stay on the trail.
- Pack it in and pack it out to the waste and recycling containers.
- Take home only memories and photographs.

How to Use This Guide

The seventeen easy day hikes described in this book rang-
ing from under 1 mile to 6.1 miles will give you a taste of
the Pinnacles, from meadows and caves to the reservoir and
High Peaks. The hikes begin from six designated parking
lots or developed day-use areas in Pinnacles National Park.
Twelve hikes originate on the east side closest to the town of
Hollister off CA 25, where the main visitor center and the
campground are located at the East Entrance, and five hikes
originate from the west side closest to Soledad off US 101,
where the new Visitor Contact Station is located at the West
Entrance.

It is important to note that CA 146 off of CA 25 into the
park at the East Entrance is not a through-road to the West
Entrance nor are there any other vehicular through-roads in
the park. Although there are no vehicular roads or shuttles
of any kind connecting the east and west sides of Pinnacles
National Park, this guide does describe two of the shortest
hikes for those who wish to experience both sides of the
park in one day.

Sections, east and west, begin with an overview of the
access, terrain, and services at the respective gateways as well
as park hours for entrance and exit. The hike summary at the
beginning of each hike is an overview of the highlights, and
the quick reference list of information below will help you
locate the trailhead and determine which hike best suits your
and your companions' needs.

Hikes are ranked as easy (flat and up to 2 hours), moderate (some elevation change and up to 2.5 hours), or strenuous (steep stretches, longer distances, and more than 2.5
hours to complete).

The hiking time is approximate, based on a 2-mile-per-hour walking pace on flat and level terrain with some buffer for photo and snack stops. Your personal fitness level and your companion(s), especially if you are hiking with children, will determine your pace on the uphill.

The hikes have been chosen so visitors may sample some of the various natural, historical, and cultural highlights in the park, and in some cases, a hike will boast several highlights through contrasting ecosystems. If you don't have time to drive to both sides of the park, you may choose the access road to the entrance most convenient for your travel needs. Since no guide to Pinnacles National Park would be complete without including a trail leading to the High Peaks for visitors to catch a glimpse of both sides of the park, we have included a more challenging hike to the High Peaks from each side of the park.

Pinnacles is not a park with significant elevation changes where you would experience the challenges of altitude. But hiking uphill can be strenuous, and the park's more extreme seasonal climate and temperature differential is cause for awareness and preparation. Summers are hot and dry, while even without snow it is not unusual for winter mornings to hover around freezing.

Trail Finder

Hikes Most Likely to See Condors
   3. Visitor Center to Peaks View Day Use Area
   7. Condor Gulch Trail to Overlook
  12. Bear Gulch Day Use Area to High Peaks
  14. Juniper Canyon Trail to High Peaks

Best Hikes for Views
   7. Condor Gulch Trail to Overlook
  12. Bear Gulch Day Use Area to High Peaks
  13. Visitor Contact Station to Vista Point
  14. Juniper Canyon Trail to High Peaks
  17. North Wilderness Trail to Twin Knolls

Best Cave Hikes
   6. Old Pinnacles Trail to Balconies Cave
   9. Bear Gulch Day Use Area to Lower Cave
  10. Bear Gulch Day Use Area to Lower and Upper Caves
  16. Balconies Trail to Balconies Cliffs via Balconies Cave

Best Hikes for Shade
   4. Peaks View Day Use Area to Bear Gulch Day Use Area
   5. Peaks View Day Use Area to Old Pinnacles Trailhead
   8. Bear Gulch Trail
   9. Bear Gulch Day Use Area to Lower Cave
  10. Bear Gulch Day Use Area to Lower and Upper Caves

Best Hikes with Children
   1. Visitor Center to Bacon Ranch
   2. Visitor Center to Butterfield Homestead
   7. Condor Gulch Trail to Overlook

8. Bear Gulch Trail
9. Bear Gulch Day Use Area to Lower Cave
10. Bear Gulch Day Use Area to Lower and Upper Caves
11. Bear Gulch Day Use Area to Reservoir via Rim Trail
13. Visitor Contact Station to Vista Point
14. Juniper Canyon Trail to High Peaks
15. Balconies Trail to Machete Ridge

Ranking the Hikes (easiest to most challenging)

East Pinnacles
1. Visitor Center to Bacon Ranch
3. Visitor Center to Peaks View Day Use Area
2. Visitor Center to Butterfield Homestead
5. Peaks View Day Use Area to Old Pinnacles Trailhead
8. Bear Gulch Trail
4. Peaks View Day Use Area to Bear Gulch Day Use Area
9. Bear Gulch Day Use Area to Lower Cave
10. Bear Gulch Day Use Area to Lower and Upper Caves
11. Bear Gulch Day Use Area to Reservoir via Rim Trail
7. Condor Gulch Trail to Overlook
6. Old Pinnacles Trail to Balconies Cave
12. Bear Gulch Day Use Area to High Peaks

West Pinnacles
13. Visitor Contact Station to Vista Point
15. Balconies Trail to Machete Ridge
17. North Wilderness Trail to Twin Knolls
16. Balconies Trail to Balconies Cliffs via Balconies Cave
14. Juniper Canyon Trail to High Peaks

Map Legend

=101=	US Highway
=146=	State Highway
	Local Road
--------	Featured Trail
- - - - -	Trail
‖‖‖‖‖‖	Boardwalk
-·-·-	Intermittent Stream
	Body of Water
	National Park
	Miscellaneous Area
	Bench
	Bridge
■	Building/Point of Interest
▲	Campground
∧	Cave
	Gate
🅿	Parking
▲	Peak/Summit
	Picnic Area
	Restroom
	Scenic View/Viewpoint
	Spring
	Tower
❶	Trailhead
⊢—⊣	Tunnel
❓	Visitor/Information Center
	Water

How to Get There

From US 101 at San Juan Bautista / Hollister exit 345 (approximately 17 miles north of Salinas and 10 miles south of Gilroy), take exit 345 and drive 7.5 miles to the Hollister turnoff on the right. Drive 3.5 miles and turn right onto CA 25. Drive 28 miles on CA 25 to the Pinnacles National Park entrance. Turn right into the park and drive 2 miles to the visitor center to pay the entrance fee and pick up a map and information.

From US 101 at King City, take exit 282B / Broadway Street and turn right onto Broadway Street. Drive 1 mile on Broadway Street to the T intersection with First Street. Turn left onto First Street and drive 14 miles to the T intersection with CA 25 (First Street becomes Bitterwater Road at the sign for East Pinnacles). Turn left onto CA 25 to Pinnacles and drive 14 miles to the CA 146 intersection. Turn left into Pinnacles National Park and drive 2 miles to the visitor center to pay the entrance fee and pick up a map and information.

About the Park

The park is open 24 hours a day, and the Pinnacles Visitor Center is open from 9:30 a.m. to 5 p.m. daily for entrance fees, maps, and information. Self-pay envelopes are available outside of the visitor center after hours. The visitor center is at the entrance to the campground and shares the wooden ranch-style building with the camp store and campground check-in counter. The small visitor center space has a few exhibits alongside the bookstore and park-related retail items. There is a pay phone on the outside wall of the building that takes calling cards but no coins. Parking and a day-use area with picnic tables, grills, and restrooms are located behind the visitor center.

There are seventeen hikes described from the east side of the park that sample eight trailheads from which to explore distinct and overlapping ecosystems as well as natural and cultural history. Peaks, meadows, gulches, talus caves, a reservoir, and wilderness woodlands await to stoke your curiosity and rejuvenate your spirit.

Bear Gulch Day Use Area, 3 miles up the road into the park, has the seasonally open Bear Gulch Nature Center, the national monument's original visitor center, in one of the historic buildings crafted with local rock by the Civilian Conservation Corps (CCC) in the 1930s. The small nature center houses cultural and natural history exhibits, an earthquake seismograph, and a topographic relief map. Maps and information are also available. The day-use area has parking for several trailheads and picnic tables with grills, drinking water, and restrooms. Park headquarters and related administrative offices and some employee residences are also at the Bear Gulch Day Use Area.

1   Visitor Center to Bacon Ranch

This historic property is part of Pinnacles National Park's newest land acquisitions and is part of the park's future interpretive program. This is a convenient, flat, skip-and-a-hop type of hike from the visitor center or campground. It is ideal for a leg stretch or end-of-day stroll with young children or folks with limited stamina, or for visitors who like to round off the park's geologic wonders with a dose of nostalgia for early California ranching life.

Start: Picnic area parking lot behind Pinnacles Visitor Center
Distance: 0.5-mile lollipop
Hiking time: 30 minutes
Difficulty: Easy
Trail surface: Dirt
Trailhead elevation: 1,070 feet
Highest point: 1,092 feet
Best seasons: Spring for wildflowers, late fall and winter for cooler temperatures. Although summer and early fall can be very hot, this hike is short enough to beat the heat on summer mornings and evenings.
Maps: USGS North Chalone Peak; Pinnacles National Park map; Tom Harrison map of Pinnacles National Park
Trail tips: This trail is open to the public but was too new to be on the park map or have a marked trailhead at the time of publication. It makes for an especially lovely stroll in the late afternoon light.

Finding the trailhead: The visitor center is on your left just before the T intersection for the campground on the right and the picnic area parking lot on the left. Turn left for the picnic area parking lot behind the visitor center. The unmarked trail begins at the gate signed Authorized Vehicles Only. GPS: N36 29.66' / W121 08.71'.

Visitor Center to Bacon Ranch

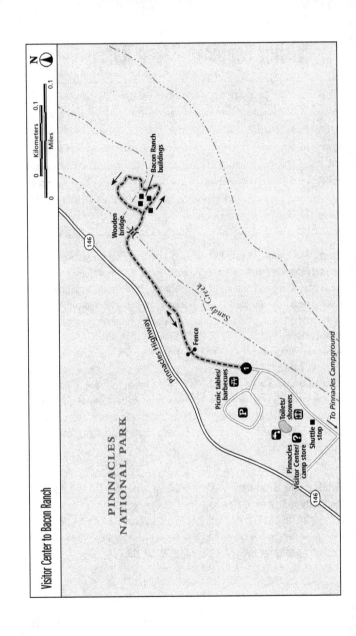

PINNACLES
NATIONAL PARK

Bacon Ranch buildings

Wooden bridge

Pinnacles Highway

146

Sandy Creek

Fence

Picnic tables/barbecues

P

Toilets/showers

Pinnacles Visitor Center/camp store

Shuttle stop

To Pinnacles Campground

146

1

N

Kilometers 0 0.1 0.1

Miles 0 0.1

The Hike

At the time of publication, this trail was unmarked. From the gate with the Authorized Vehicles Only sign, you walk on the dirt service/ranch road through the picnic area and through the opening in a wooden split-rail fence. Sandy Creek is on the right and the main park road is on the left until you walk across the wooden bridge over Sandy Creek. The creek is then on your left and the Bacon Ranch house and outbuildings are straight ahead. Wander around the ranch buildings in a counterclockwise loop. The house is on your left, and the paddock and barn are on your right. Notice the picnic table under the oak tree inviting you to a picnic, and let yourself be transported to days gone by on this early California spread. Rejoin the main ranch road to close the loop. The ranch road continues to the right for just under 2 miles to CA 25. Turn left to walk across the bridge and go back to the trailhead the way you came.

Miles and Directions

0.0 Start at the metal gate signed Authorized Vehicles Only in the picnic area parking lot.

0.1 Come to a wooden split-rail fence and solar panels (scheduled to be removed) on the left. Walk through the opening in the fence.

0.2 Cross the wooden bridge over Sandy Creek and come to the Bacon Ranch house and buildings. Begin your loop around the buildings in a counterclockwise direction.

0.3 Close the loop back on the ranch road at the bridge. Cross the bridge and go back to the trailhead the way you came.

0.5 Arrive back at the trailhead.

2 Visitor Center to Butterfield Homestead

This hike puts a whole other face on Pinnacles National Park. Rather than formidable volcanic fortresses and phenomenal talus caves, this hike, which is suitable for families with very young children or for any less-than-hardy hiker, is a pleasant stroll past a historic ranch house and through another homestead, crossing meadows bordered by rolling hills with majestic oaks. Whether you hike in the lush green of spring or the warmth of the golden fall, the landscape transports you back to an earlier California setting. A short spur on the way back treats hikers to a surprise peek of the High Peaks. You may be the lucky hiker who spots a bobcat.

Start: Picnic area parking lot behind Pinnacles Visitor Center
Distance: 3.8 miles out and back (4.4 miles with optional spur)
Hiking time: 2 hours
Difficulty: Easy on level terrain
Trail surface: Dirt
Trailhead elevation: 1,070 feet
Highest point: 1,193 feet
Best seasons: Spring for wildflowers (fans of the California state flower will be in poppy heaven in the spring), late fall and winter for cooler temperatures. Although summer and early

fall can be very hot in the open, this is a pleasant year-round hike in the early morning and evening.
Maps: USGS North Chalone Peak; Pinnacles National Park map; Tom Harrison map of Pinnacles National Park
Trail tips: There is no water or restroom facility on the trail past the visitor center. Restrooms are in the building behind the visitor center. The picnic area has tables, grills, animal-proof metal food-storage boxes, and trash and recycling receptacles. There is a camp store in the

visitor center building for the adjacent campground. Dogs are not allowed on these roads, but bicycles are permitted.

Finding the trailhead: The visitor center is on your left just before the T intersection for the campground on the right and the picnic area parking lot on the left. Turn left for the picnic area parking lot behind the visitor center. The unmarked trail begins at the gate signed Authorized Vehicles Only. GPS: N36 29.66' / W121 08.71'.

The Hike

At the time of publication of this book, this trail was open to the public but unmarked and did not appear on the park map. The homestead parcel was added to the park in 2006 and is part of future improvements per the General Management Plan.

The service/ranch road goes through the picnic area with Sandy Creek on the right and the park road on the left. You walk through the opening in a split-rail wooden fence with solar panels on the left (note that there are plans to remove these panels) before crossing a bridge over Sandy Creek to the Bacon Ranch and the buildings surrounding the old ranch house. At this point the dirt ranch road becomes your trail heading northeast toward CA 25, passing an old corral and several cattle gates along the way. Please close all gates behind you.

From here the trail takes you across meadows bordered by rolling hills and dotted with majestic oaks. Sandy Creek is on the left of the ranch road, and the paved park road (CA 146) parallels the creek on the north bank of Sandy Creek.

At 0.7 mile you pass a trail junction where another spur ranch road heads right toward private property. For now continue walking straight, but on the way back, if time permits, this is the spur you can walk up for about 0.3 mile on park land to catch an unexpected distant view of the High Peaks, looking back toward the west, before going back to the trailhead the way you came. Please respect private property; beyond this point the High Peaks disappear from view anyway.

As you continue up the main ranch road, it curves away from the creek toward a couple of barns and a horse corral on the right and an Aermotor windmill on the left. This is the Butterfield homestead. From the windmill site, open meadows stretch on either side of this idyllic sweeping ranch road all the way to the cattle guard and gate at CA 25, which is the park boundary and your turnaround point. (GPS: N36 31.00' / W121 07.87'. Elevation: 1,193 feet.) Pick a spot for a picnic and enjoy the open views.

Miles and Directions

0.0   Start at the gate signed Authorized Vehicles Only in the picnic area parking lot behind the visitor center.

0.1   Come to solar panels on the left and a wooden split-rail fence. Walk through the opening in the fence.

0.2   Come to a wooden bridge across Sandy Creek. Walk across the bridge and past the Bacon Ranch house and outbuildings.

0.7   Come to a road junction. This is where you have the option of walking up the spur for about 0.3 mile on the way back. For now continue walking straight on the ranch road past a cattle gate with a pedestrian gate on the right. Observe the signs that say Keep Gate Closed.

1.3   Come to a horse corral and barn on the right. The Aermotor windmill is on the left.

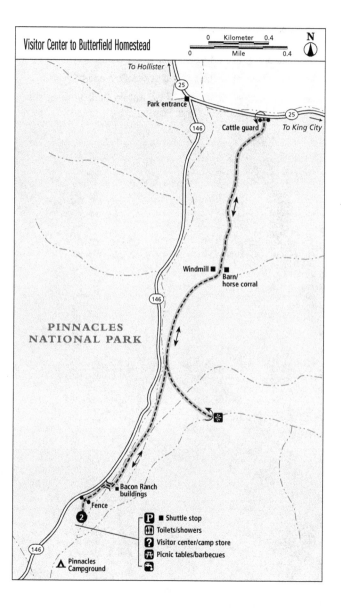

Visitor Center to Butterfield Homestead

0   Kilometer   0.4

0   Mile   0.4

N

To Hollister ↑

25

Park entrance ■

146

Cattle guard

25

To King City

Windmill ■

Barn/
horse corral

146

PINNACLES
NATIONAL PARK

Bacon Ranch
buildings ■

Fence ■

2

146

▲ Pinnacles
Campground

P ■ Shuttle stop

🚻 Toilets/showers

❓ Visitor center/camp store

🎪 Picnic tables/barbecues

1.9 Come to the cattle guard and gate at CA 25 and your turn-around point. Go back in the direction you came from. If time and energy allow, take the spur at 0.7 mile.

3.8 Arrive back at the trailhead for a direct out-and-back.

4.4 Arrive back at the trailhead if you walked the 0.3 mile up the spur for a peek of the High Peaks.

3 Visitor Center to Peaks View Day Use Area

If you can get past this hike's lackluster section along the campground road, you will be rewarded with two condor-spotting telescopes on an ADA-accessible concrete pad within 250 feet of the trailhead. From the 0.5-mile mark to Peaks View Day Use Area, it's a relaxing stroll along a creek and through pine woodland, ending with a postcard view of the High Peaks' volcanic palisade.

Start: Corner of campground entrance at Bench trailhead
Distance: 3.0 miles out and back
Hiking time: 1.5 hours
Difficulty: Easy
Trail surface: Pavement and dirt
Trailhead elevation: 1,063 feet
Highest point: 1,063 feet
Best seasons: Spring for wildflowers, late fall and winter for cooler temperatures (summer and early fall can be very hot)

Maps: USGS North Chalone Peak; Pinnacles National Park map; Tom Harrison map of Pinnacles National Park
Trail tips: There is a camp store in the visitor center building for the adjacent campground. Water, restrooms, and a picnic area with grills, food-storage containers, and recycling and trash containers are behind the visitor center.

Finding the trailhead: Turn left at the campground entrance and park in the picnic area parking lot behind the visitor center. Walk back toward the visitor center and campground entrance. The Bench trailhead is across from the visitor center at the campground entrance. GPS: N36 29.59' / W121 08.78'.

The Hike

At the start, this may seem like an odd hike since it follows the paved campground road for the first 0.5 mile, but it should not be dismissed for several reasons. The parking is easy and ample behind the visitor center. It is one of the closest trailheads to the visitor center and therefore the quickest way to get moving after the drive. Since parts of it are ADA friendly and wheelchair accessible, you may get the best view of condors in flight without much exertion. The condor interpretive panels are just 200 feet from the trailhead, with two telescopes pointed toward the southern ridge where condors frequently catch thermals. Bench Trail is an easy, flat hike suitable for hikers of all ages, and parents with toddlers who like to be carried will appreciate the absence of radical elevation change.

The trail becomes more interesting and nourishing after the first 0.5 mile, where it transitions to dirt and you walk through the gate at the wild pig fence. The interpretive sign gives a detailed explanation of why it is important to keep these nonnative mammals outside of park boundaries and how their rooting behavior causes erosion. For the next mile the creek on your left infuses new life into the area, even during the lowest flow season in drier years. At 0.9 mile an interpretive panel about air quality stations in the park describes yet another feature that makes Pinnacles National Park significant ecologically. One of the air quality stations is directly across the paved road as you lift your eyes from the information board. The stations are part of a study to measure air pollution and its effects on the ecosystem.

Just ahead on the trail, you cross a dirt service/fire road in an oak and pine meadow. As beautiful as the green and rainbow colors of spring grass and wildflowers are, the maroon of the drought-resistant scrub against the pale cream blooms of buckwheat in the muted late autumn and winter light is also a surprisingly beautiful palette.

The sandy trail rises at 1.3 miles, revealing the first view of the Pinnacles' peaks across the wash. The trail continues above the wash and traces a path paralleling the park road. You arrive at Peaks View Day Use Area and the Condor Crags information panel at 1.5 miles. The strategically placed bench invites hikers to sit and absorb the views. This is your destination and an idyllic spot for a picnic or snack and a good dose of fluids. Go back to the trailhead the way you came.

Miles and Directions

0.0   Start at the Bench trailhead across from the visitor center at the entrance to the campground and walk 200 feet to the condor interpretive panel and telescopes to help you spot soaring condors. Continue walking to the corner and trail sign for South Wilderness Junction .9, Bear Gulch Area 2.6, High Peaks Junction 2.2, Balconies Area 4.4. Watch for Bench Trail markers on the right. The trail parallels the campground's paved road to the right.

0.3   Come to the campground bathrooms (flush toilets and sinks).

0.5   The trail transitions from pavement to dirt at the hiker trail sign. Sandy Creek is on your left.

0.6   Arrive at the wild pig interpretive panel and fence with a gate. Walk through the gate and latch it carefully. There is an information board just ahead.

0.9   Come to an information panel describing air quality checkpoints. An air quality monitoring station is across the road.

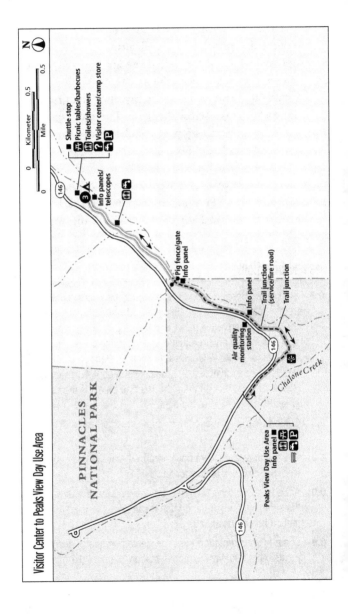

Visitor Center to Peaks View Day Use Area

N

0   Kilometer   0.5
0   Mile   0.5

■ Shuttle stop
☷ Picnic tables/barbecues
🚻 Toilets/showers
❓ Visitor center/camp store
🚶🏪 P

146

3 △
Info panels/telescopes
🚻🏪

■

Pig fence/gate
■ Info panel

Air quality
monitoring station

■ Info panel

Trail junction
(service/fire road)

Trail junction

146

✳

Chalone Creek

PINNACLES
NATIONAL PARK

Peaks View Day Use Area
■ Info panel
🚻☷ P
🚶🏪

146

1.1 The trail intersects with a dirt service/fire road. Turn left onto the service road. Shortly arrive at a trail junction with a sign for South Wilderness Trail (straight), Bear Gulch Area 1.7 (right), Old Pinnacles Trail 1.1 (right). Turn right to continue walking on Bench Trail.

1.3 The trail rises gently, revealing a view of the Pinnacles' peaks across the wash.

1.5 Arrive at the Peaks View Day Use Area. (GPS: N36 28.97' / W121 09.72'. Elevation: 974 feet.) Walk across the parking lot entrance to the Condor Crags interpretive panel and bench. This is a perfect spot for admiring this unique ancient geological formation where condors nest and roost once again. Go back to the trailhead the way you came.

3.0 Arrive back at the trailhead.

4 Peaks View Day Use Area to Bear Gulch Day Use Area

This is a nice snapshot of the lush Bear Gulch area via the sweetest mile of trail in the park. There's something enchanting about hiking up this narrow gulch laced with six wooden footbridges across seasonal Bear Gulch Creek, which is lined with buckeyes, sycamores, and oaks. Ferns, cattails, clump grass–like sedges, cascades, and a waterfall are some of the seasonal centerpieces.

Start: Peaks View Day Use Area
Distance: 2.7 miles out and back
Hiking time: 1.5 hours
Difficulty: Moderate
Trail surface: Dirt
Trailhead elevation: 974 feet
Highest point: 1,275 feet
Best seasons: Spring for wildflowers, late fall and winter for cooler temperatures (summer and early fall can be very hot)

Maps: USGS North Chalone Peak; Pinnacles National Park map; Tom Harrison map of Pinnacles National Park
Trail tips: Water, a portable toilet, picnic tables, and recycling and trash containers are at Peaks View Day Use Area. Bear Gulch Day Use Area has flush toilets and all of the above amenities. Watch for poison oak along some stretches of the trail.

Finding the trailhead: Drive 1.3 miles past the visitor center to the Peaks View Day Use Area parking lot. GPS: N36 28.97' / W121 09.72'.

The Hike

Peaks View Day Use Area welcomes you with a strategically located bench to absorb the view of the High Peaks on the horizon and an educational panel about the relationship between condors and the Pinnacles. This is a perfect spot for admiring the unique ancient geological formation where condors nest and roost once again.

The Bench Trail is named for the way it traces the banks of the seasonal Chalone Creek, and not for the "bench" at Peaks View. Start by heading north with the creek on your left. Just 0.3 mile up the trail you come to a trail junction. An unmarked spur trail continues straight to an overflow parking area; the unmarked Bench Trail goes left and crosses a double wooden footbridge over Chalone Creek toward Bear Gulch. Just across the two wooden footbridges, you come to a trail junction where the unmarked Bench Trail goes right, paralleling Chalone Creek on the west side, and the unmarked Bear Gulch Trail begins straight ahead. Bear left up the wider mouth of the gulch, where seasonal Bear Gulch Creek flows into Chalone Creek. Bear Gulch Creek is on your left as you start up the trail, but six wooden footbridges take you back and forth across the creek over the last and sweetest mile-long section of this hike.

The gulch is laced with buckeye, sycamore, oak, and cottonwood trees. Even in drier periods the creek bed at the bottom of the gulch retains enough moisture to nourish the thriving ferns and clump grass–like sedges at the bottom of the gulch. The trail meanders, climbing gradually for the first 0.5 mile up to the first couple of bridges. The next 0.2 mile between bridges #2 and #3 is significantly steeper, and if you are lucky enough to hike this trail after a winter rainstorm, you'll see how the terrain enhances the creek's cascades and rewards hikers with a rushing waterfall through the boulder channel higher up. Just short of bridge #3, the trail finally plateaus, ending your cardio workout for a while. The trail crosses bridge #4 and the employee residence driveway before leveling off at the last two footbridge crossings. At 1.35 miles Bear Gulch Creek is on your left and you come to the end of Bear Gulch Trail at the head of the Bear Gulch Day Use Area parking lot. The Bear Gulch Nature Center is on your left. If the seasonal nature center is open, make sure you stop to enjoy the exhibits.

There are a few picnic tables on both sides of the road and a restroom and drinking fountain across the road. A larger developed picnic area with grills and water is located about 200 feet to the left of the restrooms over the wooden footbridge. Follow the sign for the picnic area. Enjoy a leisurely picnic before going back to the trailhead the way you came.

Miles and Directions

0.0 Start at Peaks View Day Use Area and walk north on Bench Trail.

0.3 Come to a trail junction for Bear Gulch Day Use Area and an unmarked spur to a parking area. Turn left and walk across the double wooden footbridges. Shortly come to the unmarked trail junction for Bear Gulch Trail and a trail sign for Bear Gulch Day Use Area. Bench Trail continues right. Bear left and walk up Bear Gulch Trail toward the day-use area.

0.55 Walk across the wooden footbridge. You will cross three more bridges in the next 0.5 mile.

1.15 Walk across the driveway at the employee residence.

Peaks View Day Use Area to Bear Gulch Day Use Area

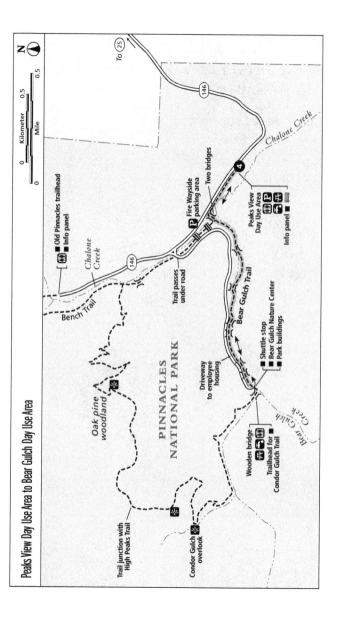

N

0   0.5   Kilometer
0   0.5   Mile

To 25

Chalone Creek

Old Pinnacles trailhead
Info panel

Fire Wayside parking area

Two bridges

Peaks View Day Use Area

Info panel

146

Chalone Creek

Bench Trail

Trail passes under road

Bear Gulch Trail

Driveway to employee housing

Shuttle stop
Bear Gulch Nature Center
Park buildings

Oak pine woodland

PINNACLES NATIONAL PARK

Trail junction with High Peaks Trail

Condor Gulch overlook

Wooden bridge
Trailhead for Condor Gulch Trail

Bear Gulch Creek

1.2 Walk across two more wooden footbridges in quick succession. Park buildings are on the left.

1.35 Arrive at Bear Gulch Day Use Area. (GPS: N36 28.90' / W121 10.86'. Elevation: 1,275 feet.) Go back the way you came.

2.7 Arrive back at the trailhead.

5 Peaks View Day Use Area to Old Pinnacles Trailhead

This is an easy route for visitors with limited time or energy looking to begin a hike with a peek at the High Peaks on the western horizon before enjoying a bit of solitude on a shady, mostly flat trail. If winter and spring have been reasonably generous with rainfall, the rocky Chalone creek bed can be a spectacle of deep blue bush lupine and brilliant golden-orange California poppies. This hike has the option of being made even easier and shorter with a vehicle parked in the Old Pinnacles trailhead parking lot for a shuttle back to Peaks View Day Use Area.

Start: Peaks View Day Use Area
Distance: 3.3 miles out and back (possible 1.65-mile shuttle)
Hiking time: 2 hours
Difficulty: Easy
Trail surface: Coarse sand, gravel, and dirt
Trailhead elevation: 974 feet
Highest point: 1,059 feet
Best seasons: Spring for wildflowers, late fall and winter for cooler temperatures (summer and early fall can be very hot)
Maps: USGS North Chalone Peak; Pinnacles National Park map; Tom Harrison map of Pinnacles National Park
Trail tips: Picnic tables, a drinking fountain, a portable toilet, and trash and recycling receptacles are at Peaks View Day Use Area. There is a portable toilet and trash and recycling receptacles but no water or picnic tables at the Old Pinnacles trailhead parking lot. If you wish to make this hike into a loop, you can walk back to the trailhead at Peaks View Day Use Area along the paved road. There is no pedestrian path, but the park

traffic on this dead-end segment of road to the Old Pinnacles trailhead is light. Chalone Creek is on your right going back if you walk on the paved road.

Finding the trailhead: Drive 1.3 miles past the visitor center to the Peaks View Day Use Area parking lot. GPS: N36 28.97' / W121 09.72'.

The Hike

Peaks View Day Use Area welcomes you with a strategically located bench to absorb the view of the High Peaks on the horizon and an educational panel about the relationship between condors and the Pinnacles. This is a perfect spot for admiring the unique ancient geological formation where condors nest and roost once again before starting your hike.

The Bench Trail is named for the way the trail was cut to trace the banks of the seasonal Chalone Creek and its wide and typically dry creek bed, and not for the "bench" at Peaks View. From the entrance to Peaks View Day Use Area, head north on Bench Trail with the creek on your left.

Just 0.3 mile up the trail, you come to a trail junction. An unmarked spur trail continues straight to an overflow parking area; the unmarked Bench Trail goes left and crosses a double wooden footbridge over Chalone Creek toward Bear Gulch and the Old Pinnacles Trail. Just across the two wooden footbridges, you come to a trail junction where the unmarked Bench Trail turns right, paralleling Chalone Creek on the west side. Shortly thereafter you walk across two boardwalks on a short eroded stretch of the trail before walking under the road overpass and across a wooden footbridge at 0.85 mile.

At 0.95 mile you walk past the trail junction for High Peaks on the left. Continue walking on the Bench Trail for another 0.5 mile and cross a wooden footbridge back to the east side of Chalone Creek. Come to a trail junction with Old Pinnacles Trail. Bench Trail ends at this junction. Before you bear right to Old Pinnacles trailhead, notice an information board straight ahead, approximately 75 feet from the trail junction. This is an information panel about the Chalone Creek restoration. Take a minute to detour to the panel before continuing to the Old Pinnacles trailhead.

The last 0.2 mile from the trail junction to the Old Pinnacles trailhead leaves the bank of the creek bed for a coarse sand path through arid chaparral vegetation. At 1.65 miles the trail ends at the Old Pinnacles trailhead parking lot. (GPS: N36 29.70' / W121 10.38'. Elevation: 1,059 feet.) Although there is no water here, nor were there picnic tables at the time of publication, there is the convenience of a portable toilet. Several large rocks here are perfect for sitting and taking time for a water and snack break before going back to the trailhead the way you came.

Miles and Directions

0.0 Start at Peaks View Day Use Area and walk north on Bench Trail.

0.3 Come to a trail junction for Bear Gulch Day Use Area and Old Pinnacles Trail going left and an unmarked spur to an overflow parking area straight ahead. Turn left and walk across the double wooden footbridges. Shortly come to the trail junction for Bear Gulch Trail straight and Old Pinnacles Trail right. Turn right to continue on Bench Trail toward Old Pinnacles Trail. Chalone Creek is on the right.

0.4 Walk on two closely spaced boardwalks along the eroded bank of the creek.

Peaks View Day Use Area to Old Pinnacles Trailhead

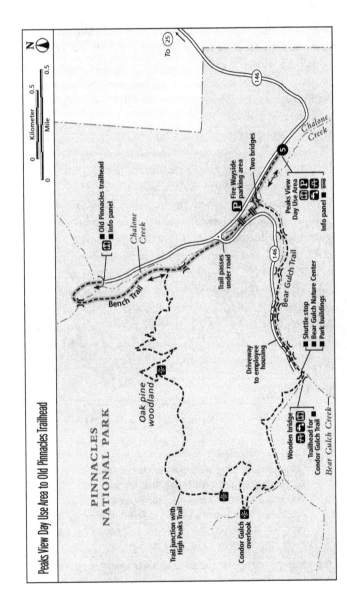

0.65 The trail continues under a road overpass.

0.85 Walk across the wooden footbridge.

0.95 Come to the trail junction for High Peaks Trail on the left. Continue walking north on Bench Trail.

1.45 Walk across the wooden footbridge to the east bank of Chalone Creek and the trail junction. Bench Trail ends at this junction with Old Pinnacles Trail. Bear right and walk to Old Pinnacles trailhead.

1.65 Arrive at Old Pinnacles trailhead and the parking lot. Go back the way you came.

3.3 Arrive back at the trailhead in Peaks View Day Use Area.

6 Old Pinnacles Trail to Balconies Cave

This is the easiest route to the Balconies Cave from the park's east side, as it is a mostly level trail with a moderate climb on the return lollipop along Balconies Cliff. The trail begins in the open, paralleling the wide Chalone Creek before veering into a shadier corridor with multiple seasonal West Fork Chalone Creek crossings. The short but dramatic passage through the talus cave requires a flashlight, careful footwork, and some limberness.

Start: Old Pinnacles trailhead
Distance: 5.2-mile lollipop
Hiking time: 3 hours
Difficulty: Moderate
Trail surface: Coarse sand, gravel, and rock in the cave
Trailhead elevation: 1,059 feet
Highest point: 1,470 feet
Best seasons: Spring for wild-flowers, late fall and winter for cooler temperatures (summer and early fall can be very hot); cool in the cave
Maps: USGS North Chalone Peak; Pinnacles National Park map; Tom Harrison map of Pinnacles National Park

Trail tips: There is no water at this trailhead. You will find a portable toilet and trash recep-tacle in the parking lot. Be aware that the Balconies Cave can be closed after heavy rains in the winter and spring season, so it is best to check with the ranger station about the status of the cave before setting out. The cave section of the trail is more dif-ficult when the rocks are wet. Be prepared to get your feet wet or carry sandals for the seven West Fork Chalone Creek crossings if you are hiking during a normal to heavy rainfall year in the winter or spring.

Finding the trailhead: Drive 2 miles past the visitor center on your left and follow the signs for the Old Pinnacles trailhead. Turn right just before the bridge at the sign for Old Pinnacles. Drive 0.5 mile to the trailhead parking lot at the end of the road. GPS: N36 29.70' / W121 10.38'.

The Hike

The trailhead is in the Old Pinnacles Trail parking lot at the end of the road. From here the gravel and coarse sand trail follows the wide and seasonal Chalone Creek on the left. The trail veers right toward the Balconies Cave at the junction for High Peaks Trail and Bench Trail going left. Just ahead on the left side of the trail is an information panel about the Chalone Creek restoration.

At about 0.5 mile you cross a narrower section of the creek bed on a wooden footbridge. The next junction is just 0.2 mile ahead on the right for the North Wilderness Trail. Bear left and continue walking on the Old Pinnacles Trail toward Balconies Cave. This junction is also where the West Fork Chalone Creek and North Fork Chalone Creek on your right meet to pour into Chalone Creek. In drier winters, like the drought of 2014, you may see ribbons of water, but don't expect a vigorous flow to fill that wide creek bed.

From here you cross the seasonal West Fork Chalone Creek seven times as it zigzags across this shady, leafy corridor before you come to the trail junction for Balconies Cliffs Trail on your right. Bear left to continue to the Balconies Cave entrance just ahead. The trail narrows and becomes more primitive as you navigate rock steps and slither your way between and over boulders into the talus cave-like tunnel. Some of the giant boulders that create this tunnel-like passage look like they are levitating above you. Turn your flashlight or headlight on and proceed slowly and cautiously through the short but dark maze, keeping your eye on the painted white arrows. The exit is a climb out of the cave to the light.

When you exit the cave, you are now technically on the west side of the park. You quickly come to the trail junction for Balconies Cliffs Trail on the right, which is your route back over the caves and above the canyon back to the east side of the park.

The trail switchbacks back and forth, passing the Tilting Terrace climber access trail on the left and another climber access ahead up stone steps on the left. At 2.7 miles the trail levels, and views open toward looming Machete Ridge in the foreground and the High Peaks in the background to the right. As the name indicates, the Balconies Cliffs Trail traces the base of the Balconies Cliffs, giving hikers a unique vantage point to admire the canyon walls where prairie falcons and other raptors nest.

A little farther ahead you may see wooden railroad tie steps up a slope on the left. They look inviting, but the sign indicates that this area is closed to hikers and climbers because of raptor habitat.

The trail gradually drops back down to the canyon floor at the junction for the Balconies Cave. This is where you close the lollipop. Turn left to go back to the Old Pinnacles trailhead the way you came.

Miles and Directions

0.0 Start at the Old Pinnacles trailhead. Chalone Creek is on the left. The trail junction for High Peaks Trail and Bench Trail is just ahead on the left. Turn right at the trail junction and continue walking toward Balconies Cave via the Old Pinnacles Trail. The Chalone Creek restoration information board is just ahead on the left.

Old Pinnacles Trail to Balconies Cave

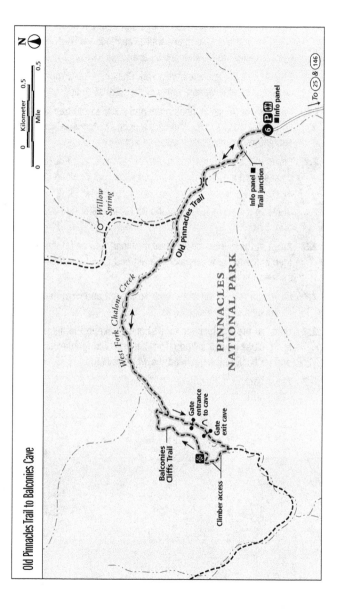

0.5 Walk across the wooden footbridge and bear left at the trail junction for North Wilderness Trail to continue walking on the Old Pinnacles Trail to Balconies Cave.

1.0 Step across the seasonal West Fork Chalone Creek. You will cross the creek five more times in the next 0.7 mile.

2.0 Step across the creek once more and come to the trail junction for Balconies Cliffs Trail on the right. Continue walking straight toward the Balconies Cave entrance.

2.2 Come to the gate entrance to Balconies Cave. You exit Balconies Cave in 0.1 mile, then cross West Fork Chalone Creek again.

2.4 Come to the trail junction for the Balconies Cliffs Trail and turn right.

2.5 Arrive at the climber access trail for Tilting Terrace on the left, then come to stone steps on the left and another climber access.

2.7 Viewpoint toward Machete Ridge to the left and High Peaks to the right in the background.

3.2 Come to the trail junction for Balconies Cave to the right. This is the close of your lollipop. Turn left onto Old Pinnacles Trail and go back to the trailhead the way you came.

5.2 Arrive back at the trailhead.

7 Condor Gulch Trail to Overlook

This trail is exposed, with a mile-long uphill huff and puff that rewards with views and a seasonal creek that drapes over the rocks at the overlook. The hike makes for a pleasant picnic destination on late spring afternoons.

Start: Condor Gulch trailhead
Distance: 2.0 miles out and back
Hiking time: 1 hour
Difficulty: Moderate
Trail surface: Dirt
Trailhead elevation: 1,279 feet
Highest point: 1,812 feet
Best seasons: Spring for wildflowers, late fall and winter for cooler temperatures (summer and early fall can be very hot)
Maps: USGS North Chalone Peak; Pinnacles National Park map; Tom Harrison map of Pinnacles National Park
Trail tips: There is water, restrooms, picnic tables, and trash and recycling containers left of the trailhead in the Bear Gulch Day Use Area. The Bear Gulch Nature Center is open seasonally. Although summers are hot, this hike is a pleasant destination for a picnic at dusk or spotting a full moon rise.

Finding the trailhead: Drive 3 miles past the visitor center to the Bear Gulch Day Use Area parking lot. Walk across the road in the crosswalk to the bench and the Condor Gulch trailhead. GPS: N36 28.88' / W121 10.89'.

The Hike

Bear Gulch Day Use Area is somewhat of an oasis of seasonal creeks and leafy canopies amid the stark volcanic palisades and chaparral-covered mountain ranges. Condor Gulch

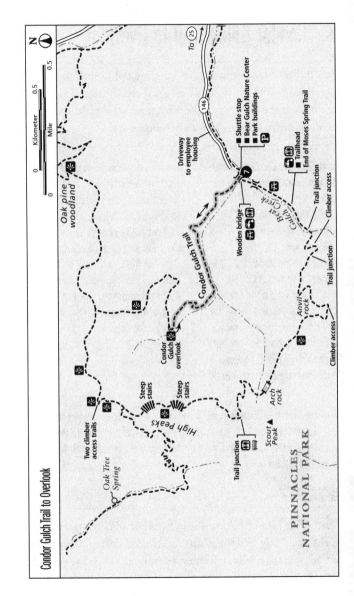

Condor Gulch Trail to Overlook

N

Kilometer
0   0.5
0   0.5
Mile

Oak pine woodland

Driveway to employee housing

Shuttle stop
Bear Gulch Nature Center
Park buildings
P

146

To 25

Condor Gulch Trail

Wooden bridge

Bear Gulch Creek

Trailhead
End of Moses Spring Trail

Trail junction

Climber access

Condor Gulch overlook

Two climber access trails

Oak Tree Spring

Steep stairs

Steep stairs

High Peaks

Trail junction

Scout Peak

Arch rock

Anvil rock

Trail junction

Climber access

PINNACLES NATIONAL PARK

overlook, at the head of the gulch above the Bear Gulch area, offers a scenic vantage point from which to admire the contrast between the backdrop of volcanic walls and spires and the mountainous chaparral foreground, with Bear Gulch's lusher transition zone bridging the two realms.

This short hike wastes no time getting your heart pumping with a relentless uphill made moderate by four switchbacks. The trail quickly leaves the shade of trees behind as it climbs up the eastern slope of Condor Gulch. The park's idyllic stone buildings on the left at the bottom of the gulch and the surreal volcanic rock sentry looming above both create a pleasant distraction as you march up the trail. You turn on the first of four switchbacks at 0.8 mile. This is a good spot to catch your breath and get a drink of water.

Three more huff-and-puff switchbacks and the overlook sign appears on the left. From the edge of the overlook, corralled by a metal pipe handrail, you have an up-close and personal view of the east face of the Pinnacles. In the winter and spring, a seasonal creek carves a path from the lush green base of the High Peaks down the gulch to a plunge below the overlook. This is a really great spot for a picnic in the shade of a late spring afternoon. Admire the vista across the Bear Gulch area before going back to the trailhead the way you came.

Miles and Directions

0.0 Start at the bench at the pedestrian crosswalk across from the Bear Gulch Day Use Area parking lot. Walk across the wooden bridge and up the Condor Gulch Trail.

1.0 Come to the Condor Gulch overlook on the left. (GPS: N36 29.11' / W121 11.55'. Elevation: 1,812 feet.) Return to the trailhead the way you came.

2.0 Arrive back at the trailhead.

8 Bear Gulch Trail

This is a "must-hike" moderate trail laced with wooden footbridges across seasonal Bear Gulch Creek, passing beautiful time- and element-sculpted boulders that tumble into cascades and waterfalls during wet winters and early spring. Even in dryer conditions, ferns and clump grass–like sedges adorn the creek bed under the canopy of sycamore, oak, and buckeye trees.

Start: Bear Gulch Day Use Area

Distance: 2.0 miles out and back

Hiking time: 1 hour

Difficulty: Moderate

Trail surface: Dirt

Trailhead elevation: 1,279 feet

Highest point: 1,279 feet

Best seasons: Spring for wildflowers, late fall and winter for cooler temperatures (summer and early fall can be very hot)

Maps: USGS North Chalone Peak; Pinnacles National Park map; Tom Harrison map of Pinnacles National Park

Trail tips: This hike begins downhill, saving the uphill for the return. Bear Gulch Day Use Area has convenient parking, a seasonal nature center, water, restrooms, picnic tables, grills, and trash and recycling containers.

Finding the trailhead: Drive 3 miles past the visitor center to the Bear Gulch Day Use Area parking lot. The trailhead is at the east end of the parking lot at the sign for Peaks View Trail. GPS: N36 28.90' / W121 10.86'.

The Hike

Popular Bear Gulch Day Use Area boasts several tempting trailheads. The Peaks View trailhead at the east end of the parking lot is the gateway to Bear Gulch Trail, one of the park's most enchanting hikes and voted one of the favorites among park employees. Bear Gulch Trail is unmarked except for the trail sign that reads To Peaks View. This hike is a moderate rather than easy 2-mile out-and-back because what goes down must come up. It boasts six wooden footbridges, a corridor of stunning rock formations to channel seasonal Bear Gulch Creek, and about a 15-foot drop-off for the beloved waterfall effect after a rainfall.

The canopy of sycamore, buckeye, and oak makes for a shady, cool journey as your eyes feast on a garden of ferns and clump grass–like sedges in the creek bed. The creek bed fans out at the bottom of the gulch where Bear Gulch Creek flows into Chalone Creek. The several fallen trees in this wider, exposed floodplain at the end of the trail make good rest spots for a snack and water break before your return trek up to the trailhead. This is one trail that seems to end too soon, and even with the uphill the "back" is every bit as enjoyable as the downhill "out."

Miles and Directions

0.0 Start at the Peaks View trailhead at the east end of the Bear Gulch Day Use Area parking lot. This is the unmarked Bear Gulch Trail. Walk down the trail toward Peaks View Day Use Area. Bear Gulch Creek is on your right.

0.1 Walk across seasonal Bear Gulch Creek on a wooden footbridge, quickly followed by another footbridge crossing.

0.2 Walk across the driveway of the employee residence.

0.35 Walk across a wooden footbridge, then cross another footbridge where the trail skirts the park road.

0.6 Walk across a wooden footbridge where pools of water feed the ferns.

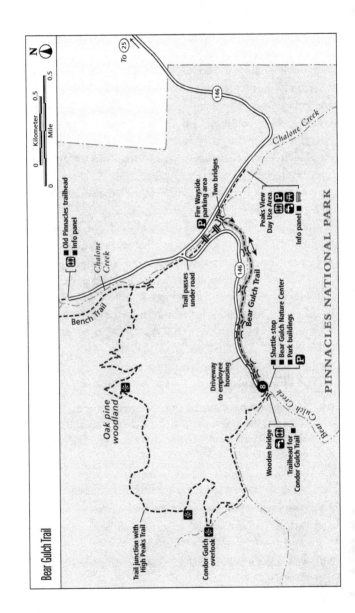

Bear Gulch Trail

N

0 Kilometer 0.5

0 Mile 0.5

Old Pinnacles trailhead
Info panel

Chalone Creek

Bench Trail

Oak pine woodland

Trail passes under road

Fire Wayside parking area

Two bridges

146

Peaks View Day Use Area

Info panel

Chalone Creek

To 25

146

Bear Gulch Trail

Shuttle stop
Bear Gulch Nature Center
Park buildings

Driveway to employee housing

Trail junction with High Peaks Trail

Condor Gulch overlook

Wooden bridge

Trailhead for Condor Gulch Trail

Bear Gulch Creek

8

PINNACLES NATIONAL PARK

0.8 Walk across a wooden footbridge where the trail leaves the narrow, shaded gulch and the creek bed widens.

1.0 Bear Gulch Trail ends at the trail junction for the Bench Trail (unmarked) and the trail sign for Old Pinnacles Trail (left). (GPS: N36 29.06' / W121 09.99'. Elevation: 984 feet.) Find a good sitting spot on one of the large fallen trees to enjoy a snack and water break before going back up to the trailhead the way you came.

2.0 Arrive back at the trailhead.

⑨ Bear Gulch Day Use Area to Lower Cave

It is worth noting that Pinnacles National Park has some of the most accessible talus caves in the National Park System. Cave lovers who don't have a lot of time or stamina for a long hike will love this trail. In addition to the unique rock-step climb out of the cave (flashlight required), this hike loops back along the volcanic walls of the gulch, passing Moses Spring, where you may spot the endangered red-legged frog soaking in the freshwater spring. Your passage through the cave on this route will be short but memorable. This hike is also a good alternative to the more exposed hillside and Pinnacles slope trails that can get uncomfortably to dangerously hot in the summer.

Start: Bear Gulch Day Use Area
Distance: 1.5-mile lollipop
Hiking time: 1 hour
Difficulty: Moderate
Trail surface: Dirt and rock
Trailhead elevation: 1,279 feet
Highest point: 1,606 feet
Best seasons: Spring for wildflowers, late fall and winter for cooler temperatures. Although summer and early fall can be very hot, this relatively short hike is reasonably shady and benefits from the coolness of the cave.
Maps: USGS North Chalone Peak; Pinnacles National Park map; Tom Harrison map of Pinnacles National Park
Trail tips: Bear Gulch Day Use Area has convenient parking, a seasonal nature center, water, restrooms, picnic tables, grills, and trash and recycling containers. Check the park website for the cave's seasonal schedule, which is dependent on the bat migration. If you wear a cap with a brim, turn it backward so the brim does not obstruct your view of overhanging rocks. A flashlight or headlight is required.

Finding the trailhead: Drive 3 miles past the visitor center to the Bear Gulch Day Use Area parking lot. The trailhead is across the road from the nature center at the sign for High Peaks Trail on the left. GPS: N36 28.87' / W121 10.89'.

The Hike

A trip to Pinnacles National Park is not complete without a cave experience. In the winter and early spring in an average wet year, Bear Gulch Creek not only makes the gulch floor come to life with green, but also gives the volcanic palisades and the caves a voice as its water washes down the rock faces and through the boulder maze.

The hike begins in the Bear Gulch Day Use Area across the road from the nature center. Turn left and follow the Reservoir, Bear Gulch Caves, and High Peaks sign. The trail crosses a wooden footbridge before entering the picnic area. At 0.2 mile you come to the Moses Spring trailhead. Walk up the trail and bear left at the trail junction for High Peaks Trail to continue walking on Moses Spring Trail. This is the gateway to another realm that reveals one of the park's many faces. Seasonal Bear Gulch Creek is on your right.

At 0.45 mile you walk through one of the park's several impressive, artful rock tunnels sculpted by the Civilian Conservation Corps (CCC) in the 1930s. This particular tunnel has the distinction of being the work of an all-African-American CCC crew. Just ahead is the fork in the trail where you turn left into Bear Gulch Caves. Turn on your flashlight and prepare to be awed by the masonry work of chiseled stone steps (over 150) that lead you out of the cave and back on Moses Spring Trail. Turn right and walk past a climber access on the left.

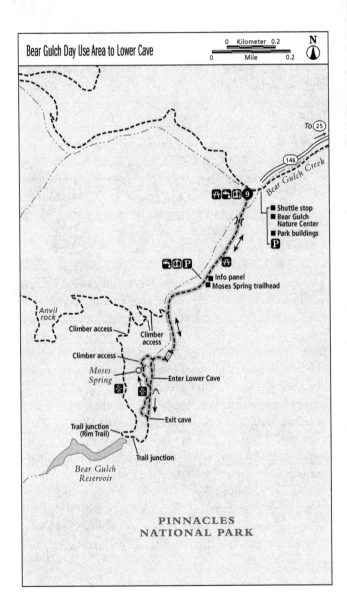

Bear Gulch Day Use Area to Lower Cave

0   Kilometer   0.2

0   Mile   0.2

N

To 25

146

Bear Gulch Creek

9

■ Shuttle stop
■ Bear Gulch Nature Center
■ Park buildings
P

P

■ Info panel
■ Moses Spring trailhead

Anvil rock

Climber access

Climber access

Climber access

Moses Spring

Enter Lower Cave

Exit cave

Trail junction (Rim Trail)

Trail junction

Bear Gulch Reservoir

PINNACLES
NATIONAL PARK

At 0.9 mile you come to Moses Spring, where a large fern thrives at the edge of a grotto; it may be your lucky day to spot the endangered red-legged frog where the spring percolates to the surface. Just ahead is a climber access trail on the left. This is the close of your lollipop. Bear left and continue down the trail back to the trailhead the way you came.

Miles and Directions

0.0 Start at the Picnic Area, Bear Gulch Caves, Reservoir, and High Peaks Trail sign across from the Bear Gulch Nature Center.

0.05 Walk left across the wooden footbridge and enter the picnic area.

0.2 Come to the Moses Spring trailhead.

0.3 Come to the trail junction for High Peaks Trail. Bear left and walk uphill on Moses Spring Trail.

0.45 Walk through the rock tunnel.

0.5 Come to a fork in the trail signed Reservoir via Moses Spring Trail to the right. Bear left for the reservoir via Bear Gulch Caves. This is where you will return to close your lollipop.

0.6 Enter Lower Cave.

0.75 Exit Lower Cave and turn right onto Moses Spring Trail.

0.85 Come to a viewpoint.

0.9 Come to Moses Spring, with the fern and grotto on the left.

0.95 Walk past a climber access on the left.

1.0 Come to the trail junction with Bear Gulch Cave Trail on the right. This is the close of your lollipop. Bear left and continue down Moses Spring Trail back to the trailhead the way you came.

1.5 Arrive back at the trailhead.

10 Bear Gulch Day Use Area to Lower and Upper Caves

Rarely does such a short little hike pack so much adventure. This is one of the many unique and distinct worlds within Pinnacles National Park, which has some of the most accessible talus caves in the National Park System. The catch is that you must be sure-footed and comfortable in dark, tight spaces. If you meet those criteria, this hike through one of the park's most extensive talus caves will astonish you.

Start: Bear Gulch Day Use Area
Distance: 1.9 miles out and back
Hiking time: 1.5 hours
Difficulty: Moderate due to terrain
Trail surface: Dirt and rock
Trailhead elevation: 1,279 feet
Highest point: 1,620 feet
Best seasons: Pinnacles boasts wildflowers in the spring, but this hike highlights the caves. Late fall, winter, and spring are cooler than summer and early fall, which can be very hot in the park. Luckily the shady corridor to the caves and the cooler environment of the caves themselves make this hike more comfortable than most for hiking in the warmer seasons.

Maps: USGS North Chalone Peak; Pinnacles National Park map; Tom Harrison map of Pinnacles National Park
Trail tips: Bear Gulch Day Use Area has convenient parking, a seasonal nature center, water, restrooms, picnic tables, grills, and trash and recycling containers. This hike can be challenging due to the slippery surface and intimidating because of the constricting conditions. Check the park website for the cave's seasonal schedule, which is dependent on the bat migration. If you wear a cap with a brim, turn it backward so the brim does not obstruct your view of overhanging rocks. A flashlight or headlight is required.

Finding the trailhead: Drive 3 miles past the visitor center to the Bear Gulch Day Use Area parking lot. The trailhead is across the road from the nature center at the sign for High Peaks Trail on the left. GPS: N36 28.87' / W121 10.89'.

The Hike

Bear Gulch Caves happen to also be the home of bats. They are "bat caves" of sorts. Park biologists specifically monitor the Townsend's big-eared bat population and their migration patterns to determine which caves to close when and for how long, so the public can have access to parts of the talus caves (if not both Lower and Upper Caves) without risk of disturbing the breeding, birthing, and rearing process. The caves are closed specifically for colonies of state-listed Townsend's big-eared bats, which are in particularly large concentrations in the talus caves.

The Lower Cave becomes a bat maternity ward part of the year when female bats give birth to their young. At some point the baby bats are strong enough to ride on mom's back, and she migrates to the Upper Cave, where baby bats become young bats strong enough to fly off with mom. The caves are usually fully open for a short time in March or April and again in October. These are windows of opportunity for hikers to experience the full cave adventure. The cave closure schedule is posted on the park website and updated regularly.

The first 350 yards of this hike is pleasantly tame as you walk across a wooden footbridge and enter the nicely developed picnic area across the road from the Bear Gulch Nature Center parking lot. Bear Gulch Creek will be gurgling on the right if you are here in winter or spring. You come to the Moses Spring trailhead at the west end of the shady picnic area. Walk up Moses Spring Trail and bear left to stay on

Moses Spring at the trail junction with High Peaks Trail. The minute you leave that junction, you enter a special realm as the trail meanders up between velvety green boulders and towering rock walls to a hollowed-out rock tunnel. Walk through the short tunnel and to the fork in the trail signed Reservoir via Moses Spring Trail to the right and Reservoir via Bear Gulch Caves to the left. Bear left for the adventure via Bear Gulch Caves.

Have your flashlight ready as you enter the Lower Cave. Don't be surprised to see, hear, and step in water in the winter and spring. The uneven volcanic rock floor becomes even slipperier in dark, wet conditions. Be prepared to walk slowly and cautiously.

Shortly after entering and navigating the narrow passage, you walk up about 155 stone steps—guided by a metal pipe handrail—to a junction. The metal gate to the Upper Cave is on your right. This is the gate that is closed and locked when the Upper Cave is the bat maternity ward. (You are on this hike because the Upper Cave is open.) You will have to do a lot of stooping and scooching in this section; keep your flashlight scanning for the white arrows on the walls pointing you in the correct direction. There are a couple of chambers tall enough for you to stand. You exit the Upper Cave through a second open gate, where you merge onto the Moses Spring Trail coming in from the left. Head toward daylight and walk up 75 stone steps to the head of the reservoir.

The caves will seem like a portal to another world as you stand on the concrete walkway looking at the long body of water hugging the volcanic walls ahead of you and the boulder cave opening below and behind you. There is an interpretive panel about the endangered red-legged frog at

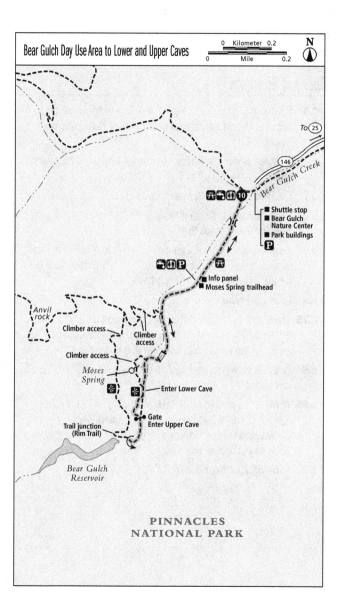

Bear Gulch Day Use Area to Lower and Upper Caves

0   Kilometer   0.2

0   Mile   0.2

N

To 25

146

Bear Gulch Creek

10

■ Shuttle stop
■ Bear Gulch
  Nature Center
■ Park buildings

P

■ Info panel
■ Moses Spring trailhead

Anvil
rock

Climber access

Climber
access

Climber access

Moses
Spring

Enter Lower Cave

Gate
Enter Upper Cave

Trail junction
(Rim Trail)

Bear Gulch
Reservoir

PINNACLES
NATIONAL PARK

the head of the reservoir to the right. Take in the view and open air before turning around to go back the way you came.

Miles and Directions

0.0 Start at the Picnic Area, Bear Gulch Caves, Reservoir, and High Peaks Trail sign across from the Bear Gulch Nature Center.

0.05 Walk left across the wooden footbridge and enter the picnic area.

0.2 Come to the Moses Spring trailhead.

0.3 Come to the trail junction for High Peaks Trail. Bear left and walk uphill on Moses Spring Trail.

0.45 Walk through the rock tunnel, then come to a fork in the trail signed Reservoir via Moses Spring Trail to the right. Bear left for the reservoir via Bear Gulch Caves.

0.6 Enter Lower Cave.

0.75 Come to a fork after climbing approximately 150 stone steps. Bear right and walk through the open gate into Upper Cave, exploring the narrow and low-ceilinged passages.

0.9 Exit through a gate and rejoin Moses Spring Trail. Walk up 75 rock steps.

0.95 Arrive at the reservoir. (GPS: N36 28.37' / W121 11.25'. Elevation: 1,620 feet.) Breathe, look around, read the interpretive panel about red-legged frogs, and turn around to go back down the rock steps the way you came.

1.9 Arrive back at the trailhead.

11 Bear Gulch Day Use Area to Reservoir via Rim Trail

This is a sweet trail that combines shade and a moderate incline to open views of striking volcanic formations contrasted by the oasis-like feel of the unlikely body of water at the foot of Chalone Peak's more arid chaparral zone. The trail then loops through an enchanting boulder tunnel and cliff-shouldered corridor back into Bear Gulch.

Start: Bear Gulch Day Use Area
Distance: 1.95-mile lollipop
Hiking time: 1.5 hours
Difficulty: Moderate
Trail surface: Dirt and rock
Trailhead elevation: 1,279 feet
Highest point: 1,721 feet
Best seasons: Spring for wildflowers, late fall and winter for cooler temperatures (summer and early fall can be very hot)
Maps: USGS North Chalone Peak; Pinnacles National Park map; Tom Harrison map of Pinnacles National Park
Trail tips: Bear Gulch Day Use Area has convenient parking, a seasonal nature center, water, restrooms, picnic tables, grills, and trash and recycling containers. Although the hike is relatively short, the cave section on the way back from the reservoir requires some fancy footwork in narrow areas. Carry a flashlight.

Finding the trailhead: Drive 3 miles past the visitor center to the Bear Gulch Day Use Area parking lot. The trailhead is across the road from the nature center at the sign for High Peaks Trail on the left. GPS: N36 28.87' / W121 10.89'.

The Hike

Within 250 feet from the trailhead, the trail cuts through a shady picnic area before reaching the Moses Spring parking area and another trailhead sign for the High Peaks. Note that although you can park here to hike to the High Peaks, there are only ten spaces, and they typically fill up with rock climbers getting an early start, especially on weekends. The trail continues across the parking entrance at the Moses Spring trailhead and information panel with a sign for High Peaks 1.9 and Reservoir Caves .7.

Approximately 500 feet up the trail, you come to a trail junction for the Moses Spring Trail going left and the High Peaks Trail continuing to the right. Bear right and continue walking uphill along the High Peaks Trail. This is the trail junction where you will close your lollipop on the Moses Spring Trail on your return to the trailhead.

Pinnacles National Park was a favorite of rock climbers long before its status changed from monument to national park. The Tourist Trap, on your right where the trail begins to rise out of the gulch, is a very popular climb. On weekends especially, keep your eyes open for climbers perched on massive boulders or dangling from ropes on the right side of the trail.

At 0.5 mile you pass another climber access on the left. Continue walking on High Peaks Trail to the right until you come to the trail junction signed Rim Trail to Reservoir. Bear left and walk up Rim Trail. The trail sits on a volcanic rock rim above the caves and tunnels in the gulch below to your left. Shortly after passing a climber access on your left, the trail crests, revealing splendid views of distant rolling hills to the east behind you. As the trail begins to slope gently downward, the rock dam at the head of the reservoir, built by the 1930s Civilian Conservation Corps (CCC), will come into view.

At 1.0 mile you reach the reservoir. The Rim Trail ends at the junction for North Chalone Peak across the dam and the signed Bear Gulch Area via Moses Spring Trail. Bear left and follow the trail down the steps cut into the rock; use the metal handrail on the right. This section of the trail winds along towering volcanic rock walls and through a phenomenal cave-like talus tunnel. It is safer to use a flashlight in this section. There is something beautifully primeval about this trail, especially after a winter or spring rain when the rock walls are draped in waterfalls. Several of the wedged boulders act as bridges over rock crevices.

At 1.1 miles you exit the cavern and pass two climber access trails just before the trail junction for the Lower Cave on the right. The viewpoint ahead showcases a couple of these stunning post-rain waterfalls before passing by Moses Spring and the first fern on the left. It is possible to spot a typically nocturnal red-legged frog sitting in the shallow water that pools at Moses Spring.

You pass one last climber access on the left and the trail junction signed Reservoir via Bear Gulch Caves on the right. Continue along the Moses Spring Trail through a carved-out rock tunnel and come to the trail junction for the High Peaks Trail. This is the end of your lollipop. Bear right downhill back to the trailhead the way you came.

Miles and Directions

0.0   Start at the High Peaks Trail sign across from the Bear Gulch Nature Center. Turn left to walk across the wooden footbridge and through the shaded picnic area to the Moses Spring

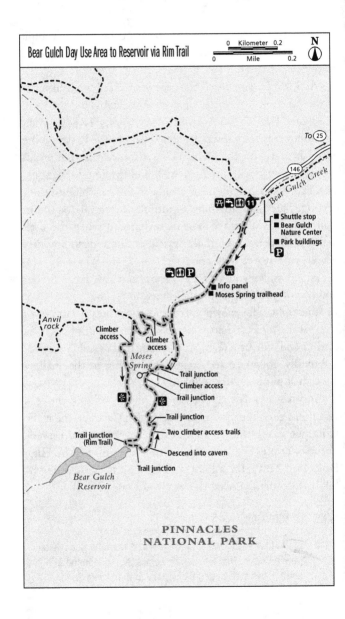

Bear Gulch Day Use Area to Reservoir via Rim Trail

0   Kilometer   0.2

0   Mile   0.2

N

To 25

146

Bear Gulch Creek

11

■ Shuttle stop
■ Bear Gulch Nature Center
■ Park buildings

P

■ Info panel
■ Moses Spring trailhead

Anvil rock

Climber access

Climber access

Moses Spring

Trail junction
Climber access
Trail junction

Trail junction
Two climber access trails

Trail junction (Rim Trail)

Descend into cavern

Trail junction

Bear Gulch Reservoir

PINNACLES NATIONAL PARK

trailhead, information board, and sign for High Peaks 1.9 and Reservoir Caves .7.

0.3 Come to the trail junction for Moses Spring Trail going left and High Peaks Trail going right. Bear right on High Peaks Trail and walk past the climber access trail for Tourist Trap on the right.

0.5 Come to a T junction and trail marker for a climber access trail to the left and the High Peaks Trail to the right. Continue walking on High Peaks Trail to a trail junction signed Rim Trail to Reservoir to the left. Bear left on Rim Trail and immediately pass a climber access on the left.

1.0 Arrive at the reservoir and the trail junction signed Bear Gulch via Moses Spring Trail. Bear left and walk down the stone staircase.

1.05 Come to the trail junction for Upper Cave to the left. Bear right to continue on Moses Spring Trail through a cavern-like chamber.

1.1 Exit the cavern, then come to two climber access trails on the left.

1.2 Come to the trail junction for Lower Cave descending to the right. There is a climber access to the left. Continue walking straight on Moses Spring Trail toward Bear Gulch Day Use Area.

1.3 Come to a viewpoint, then arrive at Moses Spring with its ferns and grotto on the left.

1.4 Pass a climber access on the left and immediately come to a trail junction signed Reservoir via Bear Gulch Caves on the right. Bear left and continue walking on Moses Spring Trail.

1.5 Walk through a carved-out rock tunnel.

1.65 Come to the trail junction for High Peaks Trail. This is the end of the lollipop. Continue walking down to the trailhead the way you came.

1.95 Arrive back at the trailhead.

12 Bear Gulch Day Use Area to High Peaks

This is one of the classic hikes in Pinnacles National Park, with almost half a mile of intimidating, steep, narrow, chiseled rock steps, sometimes assisted by metal pipe handrails on the rock faces. The scenic trail climbs out of leafy Bear Gulch up to the Pinnacles saddle, straddling the east and west sides of the park beneath Scout Peak, before looping around the panoramic High Peaks where condors love to soar. The loop closes back at the saddle.

Start: Bear Gulch Day Use Area
Distance: 6.1-mile lollipop
Hiking time: 4 hours
Difficulty: Strenuous due to uphill and challenging High Peaks loop
Trail surface: Dirt and rock
Trailhead elevation: 1,279 feet
Highest point: 2,598 feet
Best seasons: Spring for wildflowers, late fall and winter for cooler temperatures (summer and early fall can be very hot)
Maps: USGS North Chalone Peak; Pinnacles National Park

map; Tom Harrison map of Pinnacles National Park
Trail tips: Bear Gulch Day Use Area has convenient parking, a seasonal nature center, water, restrooms, picnic tables, grills, and trash and recycling containers. There is about a 300-yard stretch of narrow rock steps that are steep enough to require metal pipe handrails in some sections on the High Peaks loop part of the hike. This can be too intimidating to someone with a fear of heights and too challenging for anyone with knee issues.

Finding the trailhead: Drive 3 miles past the visitor center to the Bear Gulch Day Use Area parking lot. The trailhead is across the road from the nature center at the sign for High Peaks Trail on the left. GPS: N36 28.87' / W121 10.89'.

The Hike

Within 350 yards from the trailhead, the trail cuts through a shady picnic area before reaching the Moses Spring trailhead and a parking area and sign for the High Peaks. At 0.3 mile up the trail, you come to a junction for the Moses Spring Trail to the left and the High Peaks Trail to the right. Bear right on the High Peaks Trail for the 0.5-mile-long gradual climb before the trail transitions to switchbacks in more exposed chaparral terrain. On weekends especially, keep your eyes open for climbers perched on massive boulders or dangling from ropes on the right side of the trail.

At 0.75 mile the stretch of terraced stone steps is a welcome change to the frequently uneven rock surface as you continue to switchback out of the gulch. The green of spring also comes with the bloom of burgundy Indian warrior flowers on this stretch up to about 1.1 miles, where the trail offers a natural viewpoint toward the High Peaks to the west and an unobstructed view of the trail tracing the open ridge ahead. The most enchanting feature of this hike—and a great photo spot—is the stone-arched tunnel at 1.6 miles. The last 0.5 mile of views from the sweeping switchbacks before the bench that straddles the East and West Pinnacles at the base of Scout Peak is a prelude to the grander panorama ahead on the High Peaks Trail. As you make the last turn to the bench and saddle, you will pass a small stone building housing the vault toilets on your left. Enjoy the soaring views and a well-deserved water break at the bench.

From the bench High Peaks Trail turns northward uphill. Notice the Steep and Narrow sign. The trail begins to climb gently on the west slope, then switchbacks downhill over-looking the east side of the park. At about 500 yards from the bench, the trail starts its tricky, challenging steep sections of primitive, single-foot, rock-chipped steps and metal pipe handrails along narrow ledges. If your friends call you "big foot," the shallow chiseled steps may be more like "toe" holds than "foot" holds. At 2.5 miles the trail crests and rewards you with striking views of the Diablo Range on the northern and eastern horizon. The white streaks and blots on the rocky ledges as you look left indicate where condors and other birds nest and roost. To the southeast is an obvious swirl of eroded sediment on the face of a rock wall. North Chalone Peak and the fire tower dominate to the south. The wide rock slab at the crest is a great spot to enjoy a snack while scanning the horizon for condors.

The trail continues down more rock steps, hugging rock faces along wooden catwalks with steel pipe handrails. At 2.8 miles you come to a trail intersection for the Tunnel Trail on the west slope of the peaks. Bear left on Tunnel Trail and walk downhill across a metal walkway that bridges the short, narrow ravine before walking through the stone tunnel built by the Civilian Conservation Corps in the 1930s.

Just past the tunnel you come to the trail junction signed High Peaks via Juniper Canyon Trail Hollister Side. Turn left and walk uphill on Juniper Canyon Trail back up to the bench beneath Scout Peak. At 4.0 miles you reach the bench and the close of your lollipop. Breathe in the views before going back down to the trailhead the way you came.

Miles and Directions

0.0 Start at the High Peaks Trail sign across from the Bear Gulch Nature Center and walk left across the wooden footbridge

Bear Gulch Day Use Area to High Peaks

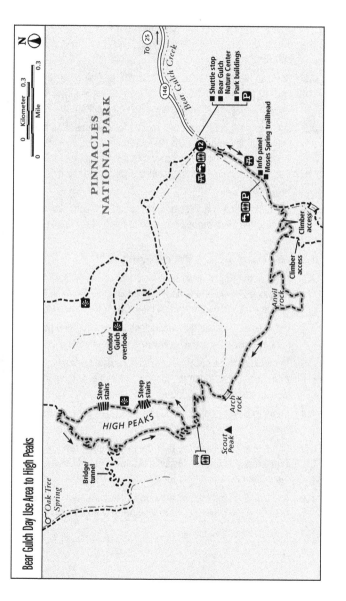

PINNACLES NATIONAL PARK

N

0   Kilometer   0.3

0   Mile   0.3

To 25

146

Bear Gulch Creek

Shuttle stop
Bear Gulch Nature Center
Park buildings

P

Info panel
Moses Spring trailhead

P

Climber access

Climber access

Anvil rock

Oak Tree Spring

Bridge/tunnel

HIGH PEAKS

Steep stairs

Steep stairs

Arch rock

Scout Peak

Condor Gulch overlook

and through the shaded picnic area to the Moses Spring trailhead, information board, and sign for High Peaks 1.9 and Reservoir Caves .7.

0.3 Come to the trail junction for Moses Spring Trail going left and High Peaks Trail going right. Bear right on High Peaks Trail and pass the climber access trail for Tourist Trap.

0.5 Come to a T junction and trail marker for a climber access trail to the left and the High Peaks Trail to the right. Continue walking on High Peaks Trail past a trail junction signed Rim Trail to Reservoir to the left. Continue walking to the right on High Peaks Trail.

1.1 Arrive at a climber access trail on the left and continue walking past the anvil-shaped rock on the right. Views open to the west.

1.6 Walk through the arch-shaped tunnel rock.

2.1 Arrive at the High Peaks bench below Scout Peak. Soak up the soaring views on the saddle straddling the East and West Pinnacles. Walk northward uphill on the High Peaks Trail.

2.4 Come to the beginning of the rock steps, with metal pipe handrails assisting the narrower and steeper stretches.

2.5 The trail crests on the High Peaks with soaring views north, east, and south. Watch for condors before descending the last stretch of the steep, narrow rock steps.

2.8 Come to a trail junction for Tunnel Trail. Bear left on Tunnel Trail.

3.3 Come to a metal walkway over the ravine and a rock tunnel. Turn left at the junction for Juniper Canyon Trail after the rock tunnel and walk uphill on Juniper Canyon Trail.

4.0 Arrive back at the bench below Scout Peak and the close of the lollipop. Go back to the trailhead the way you came.

6.1 Arrive back at the trailhead.

How to Get There

From US 101 at Soledad, take exit 302 / CA 146 and drive
0.3 mile to the traffic signal. Follow the signs for West Pinnacles. Turn left onto Front Street and drive 0.3 mile to East
Street. Turn right onto East Street and drive 0.2 mile to Metz
Road / CA 146. Turn right onto Metz Road / CA 146, drive
2.5 miles to the Pinnacles National Park sign, and turn left.
The road becomes narrower and winding. Drive 5.8 miles on
CA 146 to the intersection of Stonewall Canyon Road (left)
and CA 146 (right). Bear right and continue on CA 146
for 0.8 mile to the Pinnacles National Park entrance/gate.
Drive 0.2 mile to the West Pinnacles Visitor Contact Station
parking lot. Until now the landscape has been dominated
by California's rolling ranch lands interrupted by vineyards
against a backdrop of arid chaparral. The sudden appearance
of the towering volcanic Pinnacles on the eastern horizon
(right) will seem mystifyingly surreal. Stop in the Visitor
Contact Station to pay the park fee and get a park map. Take
the time to view the film and look at the various exhibits.

About the Park

Although the park is open 24 hours a day, the automatic gate
at the west-side entrance closes at 8 p.m. for incoming traffic

and reopens at 7:30 a.m. Vehicles can exit the park after 8 p.m., which allows for late hiking and climbing.

The West Pinnacles Visitor Contact Station at the West Entrance has restrooms, water, exhibits, and a small bookstore. It is 2 miles from the Chaparral Picnic Area and the three trailheads (Juniper Canyon, Balconies Caves and Balconies Cliffs, and North Wilderness) that will launch you on a Pinnacles National Park adventure through an ancient talus cave, offer you solitude in unspoiled wilderness, or kick your cardio and test your nerve on the peaks of the volcanic fortress.

The Balconies Cave route is the flattest access to the east side. The Balconies Cliffs route is an alternate, moderately uphill route to the east side if the cave is closed. The Juniper Canyon route is the steepest and most scenic access to the east side. The North Wilderness route is mostly flat, but is the longest route.

The Balconies Cave and Cliffs and Juniper Canyon trailheads may seem a bit confusing at first because of a couple of merging spurs in the picnic area and parking lot. At the time of publication, there was discussion about simplifying access by eliminating the trailhead at the entrance to the Chaparral parking area and making the existing Balconies trailhead in the picnic area at the far end of the parking lot the primary trailhead, with a junction for the Juniper Canyon Trail.

There is an overflow parking area just short of the main paved Chaparral trailhead and picnic area parking lot. The Chaparral Picnic Area has a self-pay station, restrooms, water, picnic tables, grills, and trash and recycling containers, but no phones.

13 Visitor Contact Station to Vista Point

This very short, flat and narrow, unmarked dirt trail is as rich in views as it is poor in challenge. It's too convenient to the West Pinnacles Visitor Contact Station to miss as you drive into the park, and it is spectacular at sunset. At the time of publication, this portal to stunning views was slated for improvement per the ADA (Americans with Disabilities Act).

Start: West Pinnacles Visitor Contact Station
Distance: 0.1 mile out and back
Hiking time: 15 minutes
Difficulty: Easy
Trail surface: Dirt
Trailhead elevation: 1,954 feet
Highest point: 1,961 feet
Best seasons: Year-round

Maps: USGS North Chalone Peak; Pinnacles National Park map; Tom Harrison map of Pinnacles National Park
Trail tips: Restrooms, water, and trash and recycling containers are at the Visitor Contact Station. Sunset is spectacular from this vantage point. Catch a full moon rise if you can.

Finding the trailhead: Walk in front of the contact station along the row of interpretive signs to the east, to the start of the unmarked dirt trail. GPS: N36 28.65' / W121 13.53'.

The Hike

If ever a hike in the park epitomized "short and sweet," this unmarked trail is it. Just 120 feet from the Visitor Contact Station, it is the most easily accessed trail, offering an unobstructed and stunning view of the unusual volcanic outcrop

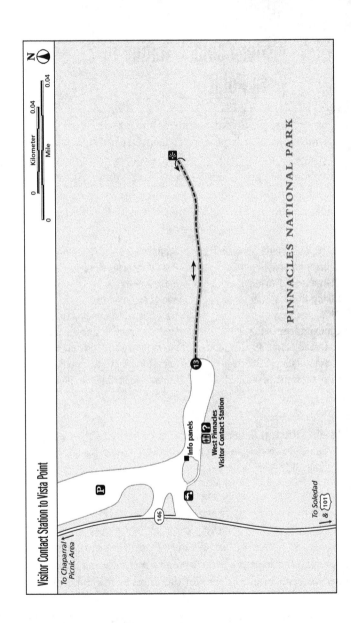

Visitor Contact Station to Vista Point

To Chaparral /
Picnic Area

P

Info panels

West Pinnacles
Visitor Contact Station

146

To Soledad
& 101

13

0   Kilometer   0.04

0   Mile   0.04

N

PINNACLES NATIONAL PARK

for which the park is named. The postcard view opens up 500 feet up the trail across grassy meadows and chamise-covered ridges. It is a great way to begin a visit in the park and offers an unforgettable last view at sunset.

Miles and Directions

0.0 Start at the West Pinnacles Visitor Contact Station and walk 120 feet east to the unmarked trailhead at the far end of the concrete patio.

0.05 The view opens up toward the rocky pinnacles. (GPS: N36 28.66' / W121 13.47'. Elevation: 1,961 feet.) Soak up the panorama and go back the way you came.

0.1 Arrive back at the trailhead.

14 Juniper Canyon Trail to High Peaks

If you have already hiked among the rock formations on other trails in the park, you may think this trail starts out a little ho-hum as you hike through the chaparral flatlands staring up at the base of more towering rock palisades. The best is yet to come. The Civil Conservation Corps' engineering feat of metal catwalks, steep Incan pyramid–like footholds picked out of the rock, and metal pipe handrails on the High Peaks' narrow ledges has an almost Italian Dolomites Via Ferrata flair that will charge your adrenaline batteries. You might even be rewarded with spotting condors on their midday soar.

Start: Wooden trailhead sign in Chaparral Picnic Area and trailhead parking lot
Distance: 4.3-mile lollipop
Hiking time: 3 hours
Difficulty: Strenuous due to uphill climb and steep precarious sections
Trail surface: Dirt and rock
Trailhead elevation: 1,389 feet
Highest point: 2,598 feet
Best seasons: Spring for wildflowers, late fall and winter for cooler temperatures (summers and early fall can be very hot)

Maps: USGS North Chalone Peak; Pinnacles National Park map; Tom Harrison map of Pinnacles National Park
Trail tips: There are trash and recycling receptacles, restrooms with flush toilets, and a drinking fountain between the parking lot and the developed picnic area. Each picnic site has a table and grill. The steep, rock-chipped stairs at the High Peaks can be intimidating.

Finding the trailhead: Drive 2 miles past the West Pinnacles Visitor Contact Station to the end of the road at the Chaparral Picnic Area and trailhead parking lot. (If the station is closed, maps and envelopes are at the self-pay fee box in the parking lot.) The trail begins at the wooden trailhead sign at the head of the parking lot to the right of the information and map board. GPS: N36 29.50' / W121 12.56'.

Note: In winter to early spring, if Chalone Creek is running too high for a dry crossing, you can walk 250 feet to the right (south) and bypass the creek crossing to join up with the trail. There is also an alternate trailhead marked Balconies Trail at the far end of the large picnic area past the parking area. A junction for Juniper Canyon is on the right off the Balconies Trail just a few hundred yards up the trail. You can see that short alternate route above the parking lot.

The Hike

The trail begins in open chaparral terrain by the information panel. Walk 150 feet up the trail in the fenced trail corridor to the Condor Crags interpretive panel and turn right. Walk 250 feet and cross the footbridge over the seasonal creek. Enjoy the wispy shade of the juniper and gray pines spread among the buckeye trees for the first mile. From here on, the trail climbs up the exposed rocky flanks, treating you to views of various element-sculpted volcanic rock monuments.

The trail is at its most challenging, unique, and precipitously exciting from the High Peaks via Tunnel Trail junction at 1.2 miles for almost 2 more miles. On this section you will use rock-chiseled footholds and metal pipe handrails installed by the Civilian Conservation Corps during the 1930s. The views are breathtaking; the trail itself is a heart thumper and not for the timid or anyone fearful of heights.

At 2.1 miles you have your best chance for condor sightings and may have the privilege of running into staff or volunteers tracking condors with spotting scopes and receiving signals from transmitters placed on the condors' wings. This summit-like area is a good spot for a picnic break sitting on a rock, scanning for condors and falcons. The descent continues to be narrow, with metal pipe handrail assists along the steepest sections.

At 2.5 miles you come to the trail junction for the Chaparral Picnic Area via Juniper Canyon Trail. There is a bench at the base of Scout Peak for a rest and two vault toilets off the spur on the left. Turn right to walk down Juniper Canyon Trail. Close your lollipop at 3.1 miles at the trail junction for Tunnel Trail. Continue walking downhill on Juniper Canyon Trail back to the trailhead at 4.3 miles.

Miles and Directions

0.0 Start at the wooden trailhead sign in the Chaparral Picnic Area parking lot. Walk across the typically dry West Fork Chalone Creek and follow the fenced trail for 150 feet to the T junction and the Condor Crags interpretive panel. Turn right, walk 250 feet to a seasonal creek, and cross the wooden footbridge.

0.3 Come to the unmarked Oak Tree Spring, which feeds the seasonal creek on your right.

0.7 The trail becomes more exposed, rewarding you with an embracing view of Juniper Canyon below before revealing expansive views northward on the switchbacks ahead.

1.2 Come to the trail junction with Tunnel Trail. Bear left to High Peaks via Tunnel Trail. This junction is where you will return from the right to close your lollipop.

1.3 Come to the tunnel built by the Civilian Conservation Corps in the 1930s. Walk through the tunnel and across the concrete footbridge over the ravine.

1.7 Come to a view of the Balconies Cliffs north on the left. Turn right at the T junction and onto the High Peaks Trail at the Steep and Narrow sign.

2.0 Start of steep rock stairs going up.

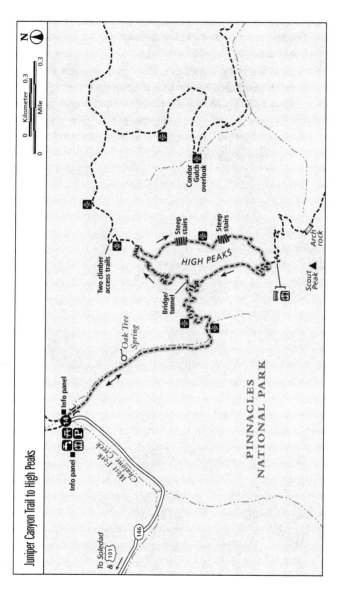

Juniper Canyon Trail to High Peaks

N

0   Kilometer   0.3
0   Mile   0.3

To Soledad
& 101

145

West Fork Chalone Creek

Info panel

14
Info panel

Oak Tree Spring

Two climber access trails

Steep stairs

HIGH PEAKS

Steep stairs

Bridge/tunnel

Condor Gulch overlook

Scout Peak

Arch rock

PINNACLES NATIONAL PARK

2.1 Come to a good condor-viewing site. Enjoy a snack and water break with a view before the descent down the steep rock stairs.

2.5 Come to a trail junction with Juniper Canyon Trail and a bench on the saddle at the base of Scout Peak. Turn right to return to the Chaparral Picnic Area via Juniper Canyon Trail.

3.1 Come to a T junction with Tunnel Trail and the close of your lollipop. Continue walking downhill on Juniper Canyon Trail.

4.3 Arrive back at the trailhead.

15　Balconies Trail to Machete Ridge

This less-than-2-mile route is an easy introductory hike to the chaparral- and rock-dominated Pinnacles realm. The trail is mostly flat, crossing a few seasonal creeks in the open before entering a shadier canyon to the base of Machete Ridge and a climber access trail junction. This hike is a good option for families with young children who cannot get a morning start for longer hikes in the spring, summer, and early fall when temperatures can rise quickly from warm to hot by midday.

Start: Wooden trailhead sign in Chaparral Picnic Area and trailhead parking lot
Distance: 1.4 miles out and back
Hiking time: 1 hour
Difficulty: Easy
Trail surface: Dirt and rock
Trailhead elevation: 1,389 feet
Highest point: 1,404 feet
Best seasons: Spring for wildflowers, late fall and winter for cooler temperatures (summer and early fall can be very hot)
Maps: USGS North Chalone Peak; Pinnacles National Park map; Tom Harrison map of Pinnacles National Park
Trail tips: There are trash and recycling receptacles, flush toilets, and a drinking fountain between the parking lot and the developed picnic area. Each picnic site has a table and grill. There are self-pay envelopes and maps by the fee box in the parking lot. The "marked" Balconies trailhead is at the far end of the large picnic area past the parking area. Unless you plan to picnic prior to hiking, it is more convenient and logical to start the hike from the wooden trailhead sign at the head of the parking lot to the right of the information and map board. The trail from the parking lot and the "marked" Balconies Trail merge 0.2 mile ahead.

Finding the trailhead: Drive 2 miles past the West Pinnacles Visitor Contact Station to the end of the road at the Chaparral Picnic Area and trailhead parking lot. (If the station is closed, maps and envelopes are at the self-pay fee box in the parking lot.) The trail begins at the wooden trailhead sign at the head of the parking lot to the right of the information and map board. GPS: N36 29.50' / W121 12.56'.

Note: In winter to early spring, if Chalone Creek is running too high for a dry crossing, you can walk 250 feet to the right (south) and bypass the creek crossing to join up with the trail. There is also an alternate trailhead marked Balconies Trail at the far end of the large picnic area past the parking area. A junction for Juniper Canyon is on the right off the Balconies Trail just a few hundred yards up the trail. You can see that short alternate route above the parking lot.

The Hike

Take the time to read the interpretive panels about California condors and the connection between Pinnacles National Park and the condor rehabilitation program as you start up the trail. You pass a small picnic area with a couple of tables on your left and a sign reminding hikers that pets, bicycles, and wilderness camping are prohibited, then come to another information board and map ahead.

This hike is less than 2 miles long, and the trail's gentle, mostly level grade wending around the imposing stone sentinels makes it ideal for introducing young children to hiking or as a multigenerational family outing. There are five seasonal creek crossings with wooden footbridges to keep the kids hopping along. But the gargantuan boulder jam forming a stone archway just past the footbridge at 0.45 mile is what gives this short hike its adventurous flavor.

At 0.7 mile you reach the trail junction for the Balconies Cliffs Trail and the Balconies Cave just below Machete Ridge. This is your turnaround point and a good place to

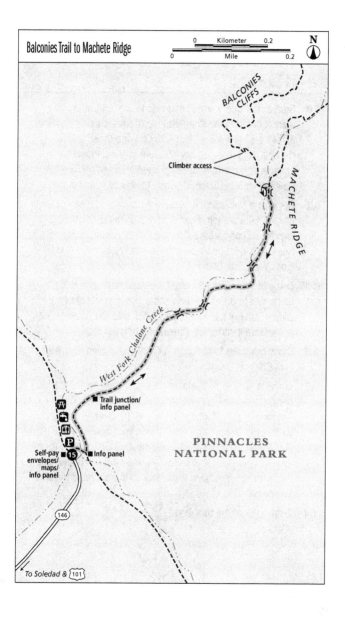

Balconies Trail to Machete Ridge

Kilometer 0.2
Mile 0.2

N

BALCONIES CLIFFS

Climber access

MACHETE RIDGE

West Fork Chalone Creek

Trail junction/
info panel

PINNACLES
NATIONAL PARK

Self-pay
envelopes/
maps/
info panel

15

Info panel

146

To Soledad & 101

take a water or snack break sitting on a rock while scanning for dangling rock climbers on the rock walls above.

Miles and Directions

0.0 Start at the wooden trailhead sign to the right of the information board in the Chaparral Picnic Area parking lot. Walk across the usually dry West Fork Chalone Creek and along the split-rail fence corridor 150 feet to the unmarked trail junction and the Condor Crags interpretive panel. Turn left, walking north for Balconies Trail. The fence is on your left.

0.1 Come to a trail junction where the Chaparral Picnic Area trail merges from the left. Bear right and continue toward the sign for Balconies Cave 0.6 and Old Pinnacles Trailhead 3.3. Come to a map board and interpretive panel. In 0.2 mile cross West Fork Chalone Creek on a footbridge.

0.35 Come to West Fork Chalone Creek and walk across the footbridge to a trail junction and a sign on the right for the climber access trail to Elephant Rock and The Citadel. Bear left and walk under the gargantuan boulder arch.

0.5 Cross two more footbridges in quick succession over West Fork Chalone Creek.

0.7 Come to West Fork Chalone Creek and walk across the footbridge to the trail junction for the Balconies Cliffs Trail and Balconies Cave. Machete Ridge and the climber access trail to the ridge are on your right. This is your destination. (GPS: N36 29.87' / W121 12.19'. Elevation: 1,291 feet.) Pick a rock for your water and snack break as you scan Machete Ridge for rock climbers. Walk back to the trailhead the way you came.

1.4 Arrive back at the trailhead.

16 Balconies Trail to Balconies Cliffs via Balconies Cave

If you could do only one hike in Pinnacles National Park, this would be the one—as long as you are not anxious about small dark spaces and do not have issues with high places. This hike offers a close-up view of Pinnacles National Park from the bottom to the top. The trail begins in exposed chaparral before entering a cool canyon and portal to the boulder-tumble tunnel passage known as Balconies Cave. You will need a flashlight in the talus "cave." You emerge at the junction for the climb up the lofty panoramic trail at the base of the Balconies Cliffs, where raptors roost, before dropping back down to the canyon floor.

Start: Wooden trailhead sign in Chaparral Picnic Area and trailhead parking lot
Distance: 2.6-mile lollipop
Hiking time: 1.5 hours
Difficulty: Strenuous due to Balconies Cave crawl and Balconies Cliffs uphill
Trail surface: Dirt and rock
Trailhead elevation: 1,389 feet
Highest point: 1,465 feet
Best seasons: Spring for wildflowers, late fall and winter for cooler temperatures (summer and early fall can be very hot)

Maps: USGS North Chalone Peak; Pinnacles National Park map; Tom Harrison map of Pinnacles National Park
Trail tips: There are trash and recycling receptacles, restrooms with flush toilets, and a drinking fountain between the parking lot and the developed picnic area. Each picnic site has a table and grill. Check with the ranger at the Visitor Contact Station to confirm that the Balconies Cave is open, as it may be closed due to flooding after a

winter or spring rainstorm. The cave section can be slippery in wet weather, and a flashlight is necessary.

Finding the trailhead: Drive 2 miles past the West Pinnacles Visitor Contact Station to the end of the road at the Chaparral Picnic Area and trailhead parking lot. (If the station is closed, maps and envelopes are at the self-pay fee box in the parking lot.) The trail begins at the wooden trailhead sign at the head of the parking lot to the right of the information and map board. GPS: N36 29.50' / W121 12.56'.

Note: In winter to early spring, if Chalone Creek is running too high for a dry crossing, you can walk 250 feet to the right (south) and bypass the creek crossing to join up with the trail. There is also an alternate trailhead marked Balconies Trail at the far end of the large picnic area past the parking area. A junction for Juniper Canyon is on the right off the Balconies Trail just a few hundred yards up the trail. You can see that short alternate route above the parking lot.

The Hike

The "marked" Balconies trailhead is at the far end of the picnic area across from the parking area, but you start the hike from the information board in the parking lot to the right of the wooden trailhead sign. The "marked" Balconies Trail merges into this trail from the Chaparral Picnic Area 0.2 mile ahead. Take the time to read the interpretive panels about California condors and the connection between Pinnacles National Park and the condor rehabilitation program as you start up the trail.

Walk up the fenced trail corridor past a small picnic area with tables on your left and a sign reminding hikers that pets, bicycles, and wilderness camping are prohibited, before coming to another information panel and map about 150 feet up the trail. Turn left with the fence line on your left to the Balconies Trail.

At 0.1 mile the "marked" Balconies Trail from the Chaparral Picnic Area trail merges from the left. You come to another trail interpretive panel. Turn right onto the trail. You cross several seasonal creeks through chaparral shrubland of buckwheat interrupted by gray pines and some juniper. The trail continues toward the canyon walls with climber access trails to Elephant Rock and The Citadel towering above on the right and the Flume rock formation on your left.

You enter the canyon about half a mile ahead and cross seasonal West Fork Chalone Creek a few more times before coming to the trail junction for the Balconies Cliffs Trail straight ahead and the Balconies Cave Trail to the right. This is the junction where you will close your lollipop on the way down from the Balconies Cliffs Trail. Turn right to the cave entrance and a metal gate. There is a gate at both ends of the talus cave. The gates are closed and locked when conditions are too hazardous due to wet weather or flooding, as West Fork Chalone Creek runs through this cave.

The Balconies Cave is one of the highlights on this hike. The talus "cave" is more of a tunnel formed by a rockslide that stacked rock and gigantic boulders while wedging some of them against the rock walls. The cave passage is only about 0.1 mile in distance but seems longer the first time because of the dark, mazelike path and slow groping required on the way down the steep, uneven rocks before resurfacing. The route is a slow scooch, crouch, and squeeze adventure. Scan your flashlight beam on the faint white-painted arrows directing you in a couple of places.

If you are using a GPS, be aware that it will probably run wild trying to locate you while you are in the cave, and your readings will be off when you exit.

You exit the cave at 0.9 mile and come to a trail junction and sign for Balconies Cliffs Trail at 1.1 miles. Bear left uphill on Balconies Cliffs Trail. The narrow, exposed trail overlooks the canyon floor as it switchbacks up to the base of the massive Balconies Cliffs. The surrounding cliff walls make a good habitat for bats, golden eagles, and condors.

As the trail levels off, you get a bird's-eye view of the Balconies Cave. Notice the spur trails for climber access and keep your eye out for dangling silhouettes on the rock faces, especially in the morning. The trail gradually descends back to the canyon floor, and at 1.9 miles you come to the trail junction. Walk across the creek on the footbridge and turn right to close your lollipop and go back to the trailhead.

Miles and Directions

0.0 Start at the wooden trailhead sign to the right of the information board in the Chaparral Picnic Area parking lot. Walk across the usually dry West Fork Chalone Creek and along the split-rail fence corridor 150 feet to the unmarked trail junction and the Condor Crags interpretive panel. Turn left, walking north for Balconies Trail. The fence is on your left.

0.1 The trail from Chaparral Picnic Area merges from the left at an interpretive panel. Turn right. In 0.2 mile cross seasonal West Fork Chalone Creek on a footbridge.

0.35 Come to West Fork Chalone Creek and walk across the footbridge to the trail junction and a sign on the right for the climber access trail to Elephant Rock and The Citadel. Bear left and walk under the gargantuan boulder arch.

0.5 Cross two more footbridges in quick succession over West Fork Chalone Creek.

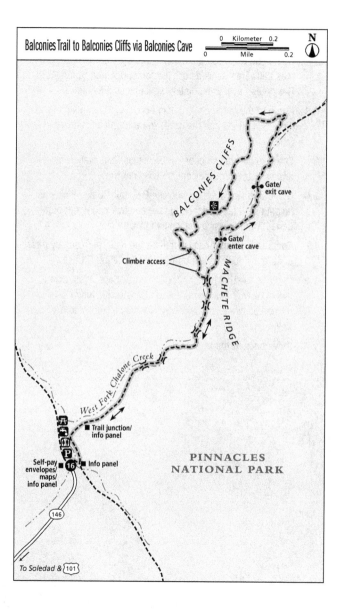

Balconies Trail to Balconies Cliffs via Balconies Cave

0   Kilometer   0.2
0   Mile   0.2

N

BALCONIES CLIFFS

Gate/
exit cave

Gate/
enter cave

Climber access

MACHETE RIDGE

West Fork Chalone Creek

Trail junction/
info panel

PINNACLES
NATIONAL PARK

Self-pay
envelopes/
maps/
info panel

Info panel

16

146

To Soledad & 101

0.7 Come to West Fork Chalone Creek and the footbridge and trail junction for Balconies Cliffs Trail. This is the junction where you will close the lollipop when you come down Balconies Cliffs Trail. Walk across the footbridge and turn right to Balconies Cave. Immediately walk across the creek.

0.8 Come to the entrance of Balconies Cave. Turn on your flashlight to continue into the cave. You exit Balconies Cave in 0.1 mile.

1.1 Come to the trail junction for Balconies Cliffs Trail. Bear left and walk uphill on Balconies Cliffs Trail.

1.6 Come to a viewpoint overlooking Balconies Cave. Pick your favorite view for a chance to take a snack and water break beneath the massive Balconies Cliffs.

1.7 Come to a climber access trail on the right, then shortly pass another climber access on the right for Tilting Terrace.

1.9 Come to the trail junction for Balconies Cave. Walk across the West Fork Chalone Creek footbridge. This junction is where you close your lollipop. Turn right to return to the trailhead.

2.6 Arrive back at the trailhead.

17 North Wilderness Trail to Twin Knolls

This is a lovely hike away from the weekend crowds. Hikers get a taste of the Pinnacles wilderness area, crossing a meadow and walking through rolling chaparral with two knoll viewpoints looking back at the west face of the Pinnacles and the North Chalone Peak fire tower.

Start: Chaparral Picnic Area
Distance: 3.0 miles out and back
Hiking time: 1.5 hours
Difficulty: Moderate
Trail surface: Dirt
Trailhead elevation: 1,386 feet
Highest point: 2,099 feet
Best seasons: Spring for wildflowers, late fall and winter for cooler temperatures
Maps: USGS North Chalone Peak and Bickmore Canyon; Pinnacles National Park map; Tom Harrison map of Pinnacles National Park
Trail tips: There are trash and recycling receptacles, flush toilets, and a drinking fountain between the parking lot and the developed picnic area. Each picnic site has a table and grill. There are self-pay envelopes and maps by the fee box in the parking lot. Plan on having a picnic snack in the Chaparral Picnic Area when you return from the knolls.

Finding the trailhead: Drive 2 miles past the West Pinnacles Visitor Contact Station to the end of the road at the Chaparral Picnic Area and trailhead parking lot. (If the station is closed, maps and envelopes are at the self-pay fee box in the parking lot.) Walk about 500 feet from the parking lot past the restrooms to the North Wilderness trailhead at the north end of the picnic area. GPS: N36 29.62' / W121 12.61'.

The Hike

This hike is a nice contrast to caves, tunnels, and steep trails into volcanic high peaks where you are hiking in the post-card. The trailhead at the far end of the Chaparral Picnic Area takes you away from the weekend fray and opens the portal to a more serene scene across a meadow, rewarded with a colorful spring bloom of wildflowers following a wet winter and plum-colored buckwheat bushes in the drier months. The narrow dirt trail laces the edge of a seasonal creek on the right and remains level for the first 0.5 mile before heading into the chaparral country, where it begins to roll in the chamise-lined swales until it crests on a ridge above a ravine on the left, briefly revealing views of North Chalone Peak and the fire tower to the south.

The undulating climb gets a little steeper after the first mile as it approaches the first knoll view at 1.4 miles. Continue up to the second knoll just 0.1 mile farther for the most dramatic postcard-perfect view of the Pinnacles' west face. Walk about 50 feet to the right off the trail to a clearing and soak up the 360-degree views of the gray pine– and juniper-dotted chaparral hills and Pinnacles National Park's volcanic centerpiece. Look eastward from left to right and identify the Balconies Cliffs, The Citadel, High Peaks, and Juniper Canyon. North Chalone Peak and the fire tower stand apart farther south in the background.

Go back to the trailhead the way you came and delight in the fresh perspective and panorama as you approach the Chaparral Picnic Area and trailhead.

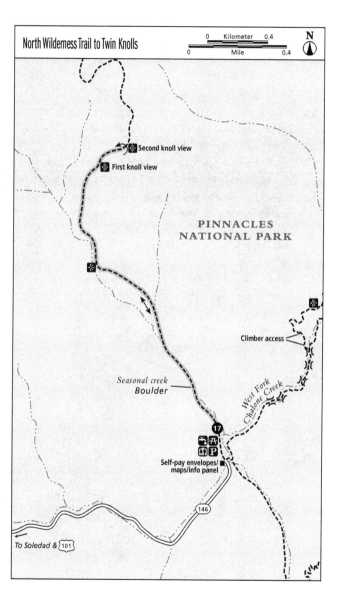

North Wilderness Trail to Twin Knolls

0   Kilometer   0.4
0   Mile   0.4

N

Second knoll view

First knoll view

PINNACLES
NATIONAL PARK

Climber access

Seasonal creek
Boulder

West Fork
Chalone Creek

17

Self-pay envelopes/
maps/info panel

146

To Soledad & 101

Miles and Directions

0.0   Start at the North Wilderness trailhead at the far end of the Chaparral Picnic Area.

0.2   Walk across a seasonal creek at the boulder.

0.9   The trail crests, and views open briefly southward to North Chalone Peak and the fire tower. The trail undulates up and down a little more steeply.

1.4   Come to a knoll viewpoint of the West Pinnacles volcanic palisades and peaks and the North Chalone Peak fire tower.

1.5   Come to the second and higher knoll viewpoint and a spur trail to the right. Walk 50 feet on the spur trail for a 360-degree view. (GPS: N36 30.55' / W121 13.04'. Elevation: 2,098 feet.) Go back to the trailhead the way you came.

3.0   Arrive back at the trailhead.

Hike Index

East Pinnacles–Hollister Gateway
Bear Gulch Day Use Area to High Peaks, 70
Bear Gulch Day Use Area to Lower and Upper Caves, 60
Bear Gulch Day Use Area to Lower Cave, 56
Bear Gulch Day Use Area to Reservoir via Rim Trail, 65
Bear Gulch Trail, 52
Condor Gulch Trail to Overlook, 49
Old Pinnacles Trail to Balconies Cave, 44
Peaks View Day Use Area to Bear Gulch Day Use Area, 34
Peaks View Day Use Area to Old Pinnacles Trailhead, 39
Visitor Center to Bacon Ranch, 21
Visitor Center to Butterfield Homestead, 24
Visitor Center to Peaks View Day Use Area, 29

West Pinnacles–Soledad Gateway
Balconies Trail to Balconies Cliffs via Balconies Cave, 89
Balconies Trail to Machete Ridge, 85
Juniper Canyon Trail to High Peaks, 80
North Wilderness Trail to Twin Knolls, 95
Visitor Contact Station to Vista Point, 77

About the Authors

Linda B. Mullally and **David S. Mullally** are a husband-and-wife team who share their passion for travel and the outdoors through her writing and his photography. He is an attorney/photographer and she is a travel columnist/author. They have been inspiring readers to experience the world's natural and cultural treasures on bike and on foot for over thirty years, with and without dogs. They share their adventures in her *Monterey Herald* travel column Away We Go. *Best Easy Day Hikes Pinnacles National Park* is their seventh book, with more titles in progress. Visit the authors at LindaBMullally.com, Falcon.com, and Amazon.com.

WHAT'S SO SPECIAL ABOUT UNSPOILED, NATURAL PLACES?

Beauty   Solitude   Wildness   Freedom   Quiet   Adventure
Serenity   Inspiration   Wonder   Excitement
Relaxation   Challenge

There's a lot to love about our treasured public lands, and the reasons are different for each of us. Whatever your reasons are, the national **Leave No Trace** education program will help you discover special outdoor places, enjoy them, and preserve them—today and for those who follow. By practicing and passing along these simple principles, you can help protect the special places you love from being loved to death.

THE PRINCIPLES OF **LEAVE NO TRACE**
- Plan ahead and prepare
- Travel and camp on durable surfaces
- Dispose of waste properly
- Leave what you find
- Minimize campfire impacts
- Respect wildlife
- Be considerate of other visitors

Because you
hike.
We're with you
every step of the way

American Hiking Society is the only national voice for hikers—dedicated to promoting and protecting America's hiking trails, their surrounding natural areas, and the hiking experience.

At American Hiking Society, we work hard so you can play! We advocate for families who love to hike, and we support communities who are creating new opportunities for your trail family to get outside. Hiking is a great way to bond with your kids, parents, grandparents, neighbors, or even furry friends.

Come with us on the trail and listen to the sweet sound of bird songs and look high into the boughs of old oak trees. We'll help you develop an active lifestyle, learn about the wonders of nature, and become a steward of your favorite trails. So grab your hiking shoes, a well-stocked daypack, partner, kids, friends, parents, and dogs— and get outdoors!

Become a member of the national hiking community
at www.americanhiking.org. Join today!

CPSIA information can be obtained
at www.ICGtesting.com
Printed in the USA
LVHW031544240322
714309LV00010B/1111